THE NEW COMICS ANTHOLOGY

the New Comics ANTHOLOGY

edited by bob callahan

Collier Books • Macmillan Publishing Company • New York

Maxwell Macmillan Canada • Toronto

Maxwell Macmillan International • New York Oxford Singapore Sydney

COLLIER BOOKS   MAXWELL MACMILLAN CANADA, INC.
Macmillan Publishing Company   1200 Eglinton Avenue East
866 Third Avenue   Suite 200
New York, NY 10022   Don Mills, Ontario M3C 3N1

Macmillan Publishing Company is part of the Maxwell Communication
Group of Companies

Library of Congress Cataloging-in-Publication Data

The New Comics Anthology / edited by Bob Callahan.
        p.   cm.
ISBN 0-02-009361-6
1. Comic books, strips, etc.—United States.
2. United States—Popular culture.   3. Popular culture in literature.
4. American fiction—20th century.   I. Callahan, Bob.
PN6725.N48   1991   91-10444   CIP
741.5'973—dc20

Macmillan books are available at special discounts for bulk
purchases for sales promotions, premiums, fund-raising,
or educational use. For details, contact:

   Special Sales Director
   Macmillan Publishing Company
   866 Third Avenue
   New York, NY 10022

First Collier Books Edition 1991
10 9 8 7 6 5 4 3 2 1

Printed in the United States of America

Book design: Dennis Gallagher and John Sullivan,
Visual Strategies, San Francisco

contents

ye olde vaudeville days daniel clowes, j.r. williams, 16

joe matt, peter bagge, matt groening, howard cruse, chris ware, lloyd dangle, mariscal, ed pinsent, mokeit, jim woodring, hunt emerson, rick geary, masse, drew freidman, robert sikoryak, kim deitch, bill griffith, art spiegelman

s. clay wilson, rory hayes, **the new punk funnies** 92

mark beyer, krystine kryttre, kaz, bruce hilvitz, julie doucet, paquito bolino, michael roden, roy tompkins, y5p5, mary fleener, jim shaw, maruo suehiro, peter kuper, mack white, paul mavrides, pascal doury, bruno richard, gary panter

lorenzo mattotti, richard sala, lynda barry, robert williams, **living colors** 128

charles burns, jacques de loustal, david sandlin

tales of politics and crime the pleece brothers, 146

joe sacco, willem, carel moiseiwitsch, cliff harper, dan o'neill, spain, mark zingarelli, dougan & eichhorn, munoz & sampayo, marti, colin upton, marc caro, tardi & grange

the forthcoming american splendor will eisner, aline kominsky, 216

justin green, lee marrs, carol lay, gilbert hernandez, jaime hernandez, carol tyler, mario hernandez, jayr pulga, ben katchor, eddie campbell, dori seda, diane noomin, joost swarte, robert crumb, harvey pekar

Let it bLeed

An Introduction to the New Comics Anthology

THE STORY IS CALLED "Zombies on Broadway," and it was created in 1982 by Kazimieras G. Prapuolenis, then just 23 years old, the son of Lithuanian immigrants from Hoboken, New Jersey, a new comics artist known to the comics trade by his pen-name, KAZ.

In Kaz's early and prophetic story, an emaciated new hero — mohawk hairstyle brought to a tease — wanders through the midnight landscape of post-industrial America searching for a way to cure his violent stomach pains.

Along the way, his path crosses with two low-life mobsters looking for rat poison to finish off a kill. He also passes a mad looking bag lady crying out for a little cheap muscatel to quench her need for drink.

In a plot line older than Poe, the fatal switches then begin. By accident, the woman ends up with the rat poison. After one powerful swig, she gags, and keels over dead.

The mobsters end up with the punk's stomach medicine. An argument breaks out between them, and one of the mobsters shoots and kills his partner. By the final frame of the story, the only two characters left standing are Kaz's hero, and a small army of sewer rats driven into a frenzy by feasting on the body of the anonymous bag lady.

We have reached a moment in comic strip history pregnant with new possibilities. As Dorothy once said to her beloved companion — in an earlier, and more innocent wonderland — "Frodo, I don't think we are in Kansas anymore."

WHERE WE ARE, in fact, is very close to the fear & loathing epicenter of the world of the New Comics. Although this world grew, like Adam's Rib, directly out of fifty years of comic strip history — you will find little of the heroic and wholesome romances of yore informing the violent and oppressive gore native to this new Someplace Beyond Kansas.

The New Comics have brought to an end certain heroic conventions which have dominated comic book writing since the Second World War. At the origins of that war, understandably enough, the comics became a largely heroic medium. Before too long, every sort of costumed super hero imaginable found themselves scooting madly after the Evil generated by the Axis powers. The comics fought Hitler, and the comics fought Tojo. And the comics have continued to fight every imagined Tojo and Hitler since that time, up to and including Saddam Hussein. Today — while the costumes have changed, and the field of battle has become various urban wastelands — the more profitable comics fight on, by formula, in the same woefully innocent, dangerously militaristic manner.

THE NEW COMICS mark the difference. Prior to this point in history, comic strips were created by often exceptionally talented men and women as way of entertaining nitwits and kids. And, while the underground comics of a generation ago were the first to challenge these limitations, the undergrounds, themselves — with a few marvelous exceptions — dissolved soon enough into a series of brand new clichéd Sexist fantasy tales, and dopester excess yarns and became, over the years, as predictable and two-dimensional as any of the old tired formulas of the past.

With the arrival of the New Comics, we pass into another world. In this new and frightening kingdom — without any known or previously declared borders — drug use is most often fatal; free love is anything but free; and the promised land on the horizon is, more often than not, merely the rising of some brand new authoritarian state.

Perhaps it was one too many Iran Contra scandals, or one too many phony Drug Wars — whatever the reason —

6

the old heroic mould has now been irretrievably broken. Neither the old Camelot romances of Terry & the Pirates, nor the Sixties romances of the revolutionary Communard, seem to work all that well anymore.

The Heroic Age is over. In its stead, nihilism — and the threat of a world violently coming apart at the seams — characterizes the intellectual agenda of the medium's most talented, post-modern practitioners. Hero tales without real heroes, the New Comics tell us, quickly become tales of abject and relentless despair.

A prophetic sense of doom — a sense of laughing at the edge — is an important theme found in New Comics literature.

More important still, the creators of the New Comics have rejected the form's earlier and easy assurances, and have moved out now into the borderless badlands where a new art might actually be allowed to begin.

This book celebrates that development. What we just might be witnessing in these pages, is — as Art Spiegelman has said — the birth of something as grand as "twenty-first century lit."

Ye Olde Vaudeville Days

WHILE A PROPHETIC sense of doom — and a faithful commitment to a new art — characterise New Comics literature as a whole, the "funny cartoonist" branch of this movement is by far the most traditional. However great the forthcoming apocalypse, it is easy to imagine screwball comics characters like Bill Holman's "Smokey Stover," Tad Dorgan's "Judge Rummy," George Herriman's "Krazy Kat," and Billy Debeck's "Barney Google" dancing on the very same landscape.

With such rich precedent, it may be enough to say that the best of the post-modern "funny cartoonists" have given the whole notion of explosive humor a much sharper cutting edge.

In his story "The Laffin' Spittin' Man," the great Dan Clowes from Chicago demonstrates why he is considered the post-modern master of deadpan humor, and why most of his characters seem like escaped prisoners from the Clown Town section of the Land of the Living Dead.

While Dan Clowes's sense of humor seems to derive from biting off the heads of live chickens, Peter Bagge of Seattle has created a legion of loud-mouthed spoiled brats who take us back to the wise-talking, early rap master shenanigans of the original Katzenjammers, and The Yellow Kid. They also take us forward to The Simpsons. Clowes and Bagge are both outstanding contributors to the current generation of New Vaudevillians.

Like archaeologists opening an Etruscan tomb, New York artists Drew Friedman and Art Spiegelman have both drawn inspiration from a careful re-examination of some of the more hideous personalities and artifacts of 1950s American pop culture.

THE LAST THING I GLIMMED BEFORE SLUGGING THE CARPET WITH MY SNIFFER WAS THE DOLL'S PUSS —WITH POTATOHEAD!

8

ANTIC GRAMMAR

Art Spiegelman's post-modern midget detective, "Ace Hole" (above) is central to a screwball tradition inspired by the tonic "hoo-hah" of <u>Mad</u>'s Harvey Kurtzman (opposite top); and extends back in time to the legendary T.A.D. (opposite bottom), who coined first language for the realm.

One of the New Comic's most brilliant intellectuals, Art Spiegelman has created "Ace Hole, Midget Detective," a particular gem. In "Ace Hole," he humorously insists that to have a truly new comic art, the lessons of Pablo Picasso and the lessons of Chester Gould both must be put into play.

Back in the 1970s Spiegelman co-edited with Bill Griffith, the creator of Zippy the Pinhead, a wonderful slapstick comics magazine called *Arcade*. As featured in this anthology, Griffith's "Dollboy" also dates back to that period. On re-reading, "Dollboy" seems profoundly Chaplinesque. By the way, the doll never really died, of course. He continues to sit clumsily on Griffith's lap today in the form of goofy old Zippy.

Kim Deitch was also a regular contributor to the early *Arcade*. His "Famous Frauds" series first demonstrated Deitch's ongoing fascination with the grotesque and macabre worlds of vaudeville, the carnival life, and Hollywood, in the first decades of this century.

England's Hunt Emerson is widely considered the best "funny" cartoonist currently working in the British Isles. Emerson has been profoundly influenced by the American underground comix movement of the 1960s; and yet, as "Buster in Mouth City," clearly demonstrates the ultimate source of this humor is undoubtedly the early silent films of Arbuckle, Chaplin, Keaton, Langdon and Lloyd.

It is a particular pleasure to introduce in the pages of this anthology the first English language appearances of both "Public Utilities" by France's Francis Masse, and "An Unexpected Journey" by Spain's Javier Mariscal.

It was the English editor Paul Gravett who first noted that Masse's unnamed, mysterious, bowler-capped main character evokes Magritte, and seems to have wandered directly out of a play by Samuel Beckett. Mariscal, on the other hand, seems to be coming from a far more innocent palace of the heart — a land where the power and wonders of Kandisky meets the pratfalls of Disney. Mariscal's Firmin and Piker stories — of which "An Unexpected Journey" is a previously untranslated episode — is Spain's most miraculous, contemporary, New Comics strip.

However more complex, and multi-dimensional, their design, New Comics "funny cartoonists" are the direct heirs to a marvellous slapstick tradition, now well over a hundred years old.

The New Punk Funnies

THE PUNK FUNNIES wing of the New Comics movement is almost unprecedented in terms of American comic strip history. While exaggeration has always been an essential element in comic art, the sense of violence and the grotesque found in the New Punk Funnies picks up from William Gaine's E.C. horror stories of the 1950s — as well as the work of Basil Wolverton — and then moves out into a hyperspace all of its own. In the end you probably have to go all the way back to the major work of those two wonderful Central European funsters — surehanded "Pete" Brueghal, and Mr. Chuckles himself, merry old "Heiney" Bosch — to find real precedent for this work. It is quite clear that the authors of the New Punk Funnies march to the beat of their very own conga drum. These authors are the

9

CHICKEN FANCIERS AT THE MARKET

APOCALYPSE NOW

Mark Beyer's "Amy" (above) surveys the fantastic and grotesque world of Basil Wolverton's imagination (opposite top), and the truly bizarre anti-Axis spring catalog comics of Boris Artzybasheff (opposite bottom), as the Comedy of Fear continues to unfold.

Weathermen of the New Comics Movement. From the looks of the evidence gathered in this section, for the next decade or so, it seems like we are in for more rain.

If you like, perhaps we can blame the whole thing on Robert Crumb. Published in Northern California at the tail end of the Underground Era, Robert Crumb's *Weirdo* magazine provided an early forum for many of these new punk artists. The work of Roy Tompkins, Michael Roden, Krystine Kryttre, and Mary Fleener, as well as that of underground "ugly art" pioneers such as Wilson, Hayes, and Robert Williams —were regularly featured in *Weirdo*, particularly after Peter Bagge became the magazine's editor in the mid-1980s.

While *Weirdo* was examining the joys of the new punk funnies for itself back in the mid-1980s, Art Spiegelman and Francoise Mouly in New York were opening the pages of their own *Raw* magazine to comparable, if even more troubled and demanding talents. Kaz's zombie-ridden post-industrial urban wastelands; Mark Beyer's angst-ridden "Amy and Jordan" tales; and Gary Panter's powerful "Jimbo" sagas were all featured in the early issues of *Raw* .

By the end of the decade, punk or ugly art had become an international phenomena. Inspired by Panter, Maruo Suehiro's own violent and outrageous comic strips became something of a scandal in his own native Tokyo, Japan. Julie Doucet's carefully crafted, sexually explicit autobiographical fantasies provided a window into punk culture in far off Montreal. And Bruno Richard and Pascal Doury — both in collaboration, and by themselves — seemed to head the list of a fascinating new generation of enormously talented punk strip artists practicing their own particular brand of subversion from the cobblestone streets of Paris, France.

Of the many branches and tributaries of New Comics literature, the punk funnies of the 1980s succeeded in reaching furthest into the subconscious and violent dreamscapes of our own most troubled age.

Politics & Crime

REJECTING THE FORMULA heroism of the super-hero comic book, and building a body of work instead on the psychologically intense war and crime stories associated with William Gaine's E.C. publications in 1950s, New Comics writers have already created some of the most politically sophisticated, and realistic crime and suspense thrillers in the history of the graphic adventure tale.

Unlike their colleagues working in the super-hero genre, New Comics writers are opposed to jingoism, even in its most seductive forms. In this regard it is significant to note that, during the recent Gulf War crisis, the syndicated cartoons of New Comics artists Bill Griffith, Lynda Barry, and Matt Groening remained just about the only section of the daily newspaper where the massive bombing campaign in Iraq was regularly called into question. Many of the New Comics artists grew up during the period of Viet Nam. The real lessons of that war continue to inform the way in which they chosen to write crime and political terror stories today.

In "London's Changed" by Gary and Warren Pleece — a story which echos the fate of too many Viet Nam veterans —a lonely soldier returns from the battlefields of World War One only to find that Great Britain has forgotten to make a place for him in the aftermath. In "Durruti" by Spain Rodriquez we experience the tragic death of one of the forgotten heroes of the Spanish Civil War.

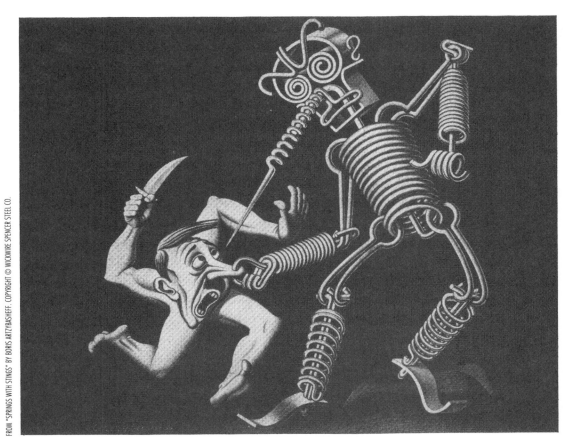

12

WE DID IT

Jacques Tardi's contemporary French _noir_ comics (above) extend an ongoing, criminal history of the 20th century which includes the early, far more innocent, 1930 promptings of Roy Crane (opposite left), and the classic 1950 political horror tales of the brilliant Bernard Krigstein (opposite right).

While Spain and the Pleece Brothers have chosen to tell their tales through the eyes of a first-person narrator, artists of the caliber of America's Joe Sacco, Canada's Carel Moiseiwitsch, and France's Willem — formerly the lead cartoonist for France's weekly political newspaper, _Liberation_ — employ a documentary style to reconstruct actual historical incidents, a form of new comics writing which some critics have already dubbed "the new graphic journalism." Willem's "Jerusalem," in particular, is a remarkable achievement — a wordless retelling of the recent terrorist history of the Mideast which gathers momentum soley through the artful juxtaposition of familiar news photo images.

Just as Willem is the world's leading master of the new graphic journalism, other new comics writers from France have broken new ground in portraying what Raymond Chandler once called "The Simple Act of Murder." In the work of Jacques Tardi, Marc Caro, and Jacques Loustal, we encounter the French _roman noir_ school of comic strip writing. The best of these strips are state-of-the-art, in terms of graphic literature today.

The French, of course, are not alone in this emphasis. The work of Seattle's Mark Zingarelli, Spain's Marti Ribera, and Argentina's remarkable Munoz & Sampayo (now living in exile in Italy) begins where the great E.C. war and adventure tales of the 1950s left off, and manages to take New Comics crime writing to the very cutting edge. Like the more imagistic, yet equally dark poetic works of their rebellious young cousins — the punks — the New Comics crime writers have created a profoundly subversive, prophetic body of work which speaks directly to the dark and corrupted political heart of our time.

The Forthcoming American Splendor

THE CLAIM THAT the New Comics represent a vital new branch of contemporary literature rests largely on the basis of the variety of autobiographical writings found in the final section of the New Comics Anthology. Although young writers have long been advised to write through their own unique body of experience, few comics writers — with the noble exception of the great Will Eisner — have ever bothered to follow this primary literary injunction all that carefully before. In creating a new graphic literature upon these grounds, New Comics writers have effectively transformed this particular branch of New Comics literature into one of the most provocative literary cross-currents of our time. Reading these stories today, we are present at the birth of a vital moment in comics history — a moment when a beloved form of popular _entertainment_ sheds its last cocoon, and is transformed at last into a daring new pop _art form_.

It should also come as no surprise to learn that the overwhelming number of new comics writers working today in alternative biographical and autobiographical forms are women. Women were by and large excluded from the older "heroic" worlds of the comics; even Wonder Woman was drawn by a man who apparently had a sexual fetish for whips, ropes and chains.

New Comics Literature is, in the main, decidedly feminist. Whether it be the working woman sensibility which informs the stories of Lee Marrs and Carol Tyler; the avante garde and experimental worlds of Carol Lay and the late Dori Seda; the smart, sexy, middle class cosmopolitan tales being created by Aline Kominsky and Dianne Noomin; or the brilliant narrative

skills of Lynda Barry, feminism has entered the world of the New Comics primarily through the agency of these stories.

Mario, Gilbert and Jaime Hernandez are three young Mexican American brothers from Southern California who have also turned the New Comics movement on its ears. It may be said that Mario is more the poet, Gilbert the mythologist, and Jaime the urban realist; but the simple fact is that each of the Hernandez Brothers has returned in their writings to the truth of life in their own ancestral communities. Because of the genius of the Hernandez Brothers, New Comics writing is no longer the exclusive concern of Anglos writers.

The sense of a distinct ethnic neighborhood heritage is also a dominant element in the pub stories of Scotland's Eddie Campbell, and the lower East Side immigrant tales of New York's Ben Katchor. The work of Campbell and Katchor can be seen, moreover, as an extension of the working class environments of Cleveland Ohio where the great Harvey Pekar first introduced the autobiographical, social realist concerns which have now been absorbed by the entire New Comics movement.

Particularly as drawn by his close friend, Robert Crumb, Pekar's Cleveland stories began to appear in his own, self-published comic book, *American Splendor*, back in 1976. The best of these tales long ago established Pekar as one of the finest short story writers of our age. That a writer

SUNDAY MORNING

HMMM... THAT WOMAN FROM THAT BIG PUBLISHER NEVER GOT BACK T'ME. GUESS SHE WASN'T SERIOUS; PROB'LY WANTED A FREE BOOK OR WAS TOO LAZY T' LOOK FOR MY STUFF ON THE STANDS OR SUMP'N.

with Pekar's obvious literary skills turned to graphic literature as a favored medium for self-expression served to inspire other real writers and artists to begin to collaborate along these lines.

Along with Art Spiegelman's *Maus* — a miraculous graphic novel which proved too rich to excerpt for this anthology — Pekar's *American Splendor* short stories represent the crowning literary achievement of the New Comics movement to date.

WHETHER REINVENTING THE old slapstick tradition, or exploring new and dangerous cosmologies of the mind, the New Comics artists represent the most skilled generation of illustrators ever to work in the comics form. Whether spinning new political or auto-biographical tales, the New Comics writers have helped to make graphic literature one of the most challenging new art forms today.

The road seems wide open up ahead.

14

SONGS OF MYSELF

Harvey Pekar and Robert Crumb's "American Splendor" short stories (above) echo the earlier, Midwestern populist essays of J.R. Williams (opposite top), and the poetic naturalism of the Ohio Valley's Frank King (opposite bottom).

IN CLOSING I SHOULD like to acknowledge the help of artists and writers Dan O'Neill, Dean Mullaney, Kat Yronwode, Spain, Ron Turner, Clay Wilson, and Robert Crumb, for sharing with me, over the years, months, and weeks leading up to the creation of this anthology so many of their own unique insights into the possibilities of this new form.

I also enjoyed enormously the gathering experience itself, as that became the the occasion for so many warm and friendly introductory phone conversations over the course of this past year. The memory of late night yaps and Saturday morning guffaws with the likes of Dan Clowes, Peter Bagge, Rick Geary, Bill Griffith, Drew Freidman, Mark Beyer, Kaz, Krystine Kryttre, Mary Fleener, Mark Zingarelli, Will Eisner, Justin Green, Mario Hernandez, Diane Noomin, Eddie Campbell, Harvey Pekar, and, in particular, my new pinball wizard friend, Art Spiegelman, helped make this book a constant delight to put together, end to end.

I should also like to thank old writer friends Warren Hinckle, Pete Hamill, T.J. English, and Ishmael Reed for helping me to sort out and begin to articulate some sense of meaning from the constant swirl of all these new impressions. The oversights which exist in this collection are soley my responsibility. I only regret that I did not plan for an additional hundred pages to include even more writers in what is, nonetheless, the largest collection of New Comics literature ever assembled. Oh well, as Jimmy Durante once said, "There's always the sequel...."

This book has also profited a great deal from the research expertise of Mark Stichman and his associates at Comic Relief in Berkeley, and Eric Gilbert at Last Gasp Comics in San Francisco. I am also indebted to my agent, Norman Kurz of the Barbara Lowenstein Agency, and to my editor, Wendy Batteau, and her associates at Collier and Macmillan. In conclusion I should like to dedicate this book to the memory of two brilliant Bay Area comic spirits, Dori Seda and Artie Mitchell. What a privilege it was to share the warmth and laughter of their company over the years.

Bob Callahan
Oakland
March, 1991

the new comics movement includes a number of brilliant contemporary "funny" cartoonists whose roots can be traced back to the earliest screwball comic strips produced in this century. the situations have clearly changed; yet, at source, the laughter seems very much the same.

Ye oLde vaudeviLLe dayS

18 THE LAFFIN' SPITTIN' MAN
by Daniel Clowes

Fresh from the pages of Clowes's own *Eightball* comic book, Lloyd Llewellyn encounters another travelling salesman with a bag of tricks as deep as his own.

24 THE QAALUDE FAMILY
by J.R. Williams

From the woods of the Pacific Northwest, J.R. Williams provides searing insight into the psychic life of your typical American nuclear-fried family.

27 MY PARENTS
by Joe Matt

In a glowing tribute to the virtues of his own early home life, Toronto's Joe Matt creates a one page novel in just 27 tiny panels.

28 IN MY ROOM
by Peter Bagge

An early classic from the contemporary master of spoiled brat humor.

33 CAN WE GO TO A GAY BAR TONIGHT?
by Matt Groening

The cartoon which blew the lid off the story about just how many fez-wearing gay midgets you are liable to find at your average saturday evening Seattle house party.

34 RAISING NANCIES
by Howard Cruse

The talented author of "Dancin' Nekkid with the Angels" at his best — if only Ernie Bushmiller had known he had a fan base like this.

37 JIMMY CORRIGAN
by Chris Ware

The brilliant young Austin, Texas talent demonstrates how cleanly he has mastered the lessons of panelled pages, and early C.C. Beck comic books.

38 WE ALL LIVE ON A GARBAGE BARGE
by Lloyd Dangle

The popular new San Francisco comics whiz explains just what it was he learned from George Bush, and the Contras.

41 AN UNEXPECTED JOURNEY
by Mariscal

Firmin and Piker have problems getting out of town — the first English language reproduction of this unique episode from Spain's most respected ongoing comic strip.

45 PRIMITIF
by Ed Pinsent

Resembling nothing so much as a lost episode from Mayan mythology, England's Ed Pinsent introduces the strange world of Primitif, a rather odd warrior.

48 THE TWIDDLERS
by Mokeit

One of France's finest young New Comics artists creates a fascinating allegory for the rise of Neo-Nazism in contemporary Europe.

51 FRANK AND MANHOG
by Jim Woodring

The author of the brilliant comic book "Jim," on how Gods are often born.

55 BUSTER IN MOUTH CITY
by Hunt Emerson

England's most popular "funny cartoonists" dissects an unusual pratfall.

59 FAREWELL TO CHARLIE CHAPLIN
by Rick Geary

One of the most charming of all the New Comics masters reconstructs a very strange grave robbery.

62 PUBLIC UTILITIES
by Francis Masse

Scarecrows, public utility poles, and not a small amount of French surrealism define the first English language reproduction of this early, and favored story by France's inimitable — ultimately indescribable — Francis Masse.

64 TENSION WOMAN
by Joe Schwind

Three previously unconstructed short stories by the master of the American comic strip collage.

67 DOLLBOY
by Bill Griffith

A truly haunting — and prophetic — early tale by the creator of "Zippy the Pinhead."

72 INDETERMINACY
by Robert Sikoryak

Raw Magazine's Bob Sikoryak recasts the adventures of some of the medium's classics in a more anxiety-ridden, post-modern context.

76 THE ADVENTURES OF DON CARLOS BALMORI
by Kim Deitch

In this first of a series of comic strips celebrating "Famous Frauds," the brilliant Kim Deitch plays homage to one of the more bizarre scams of recent Mexican history.

80 LAUGH MAKERS
by Drew Freidman

Neglected moments in pop culture history — by the genius young cartoonist Robert Crumb has called "The Robert Crumb of the Eighties."

84 ACE HOLE, MIDGET DETECTIVE
by Art Spiegelman

Dick Tracy meets Pablo Picasso in this early comic masterpiece by the author of "Maus," and co-founder of *Raw Magazine*.

≥Sob≥ My HUSBAND! ≥Sob≥ He KNOWS EVERY-THING! ≥Sob≥

Now LISSEN HERE ...You NEVER SAID ANYTHING about a--

You don't understand ≥Sob≥ He's not like other men... He's a TRAVELING NOVELTY SALESMAN! He's a NUT! He's CAPABLE of ANYTHING!

...GET OUT OF TOWN FAST!

Okay, so what am I doing in a glorified stoplight like Schneiderville wasting my time with a chick who on a good day looks like a young Thelma Ritter and who didn't even have the common courtesy to tell me that she was married to a lunatic when she took advantage of me? A good question that deserves an answer-- Unfortunately I only have 6 pages in this issue so you're gonna have to take my word for it...

Hiya, Mr. Llewellyn! How's your ol' straw hat? Put 'er there!

GAAA!

BUZZZ

HAW HAW HAW! Glad to know you, pal...I'm Emmett Ceeley ...LOUISE'S HUSBAND!

Do you enjoy a good laugh, Mr. Llewellyn? I sure do!

...Do you like me? Some people find me abrasive! AM I ABRASIVE? AM I ANNOYING?

...Oh God... M-My life has ...turned to $hit! ≥Sob≥

≥Whimper≥ ≥SNORT≥

19

I-It wasn't MY fault...
I-It was SUICIDE... I
TRIED to STOP HIM...
...I-If I wait in
my room until the
whole thing blows over,
maybe-- OHOH,
THE COPS!

...If I was a decent,
honorable American with
faith in justice and fair
play I'd go tell them the
truth and take my
chances...
IF!

I need an
alibi... what
was I doing this
evening...
HMMMM...

Hey buddy! A
double-shot of
Slow Joe Crow
and bring the
young lady a
fresh one!

Right
away,
sir!

Thanks... y'got
another cigarette?

You bet,
Honey!

That's a lovely shade
of lipstick you're
wearing, miss!

::Grunt::

BAM!

GODDAMMIT!
::Coff! Coff!::
I SUPPOSE
YOU THINK
THAT'S
FUNNY!?
Coff!
Coff!
Coff!

NO!
I-I mean
I'm SORRY!
I-I don't know
how it could
have
happened...

...I bought these
cigarettes in the
lobby this mor--

BRAAP!

21

WELL, TAKE A ♣✖✖♦!! LOOK AROUND!! THE YARD IS A ⚡⊗✝@!! WRECK!!
--SO?? HIRE A ♣✖✖♦!! GARDENER!!
GOD--YOU MIGHT BE RIGHT--IT'S AN IMPOSSIBLE JOB--THERE'S NOT EVEN ONE PLANT THAT'S STILL SLIGHTLY GREEN...
--HEY, POP!! LOOK! THERE'S A PLANT OVER THERE THAT'S STILL ALIVE!!!
WELL, I'LL BE @☆€✖!!! IT'S STILL GOT LEAVES--IT'S EVEN GOT SOME FLOWERS ON IT!!
WHAT'S THAT LITTLE, SHINY BROWN THING? IT LOOKS KINDA LIKE A.... A.....
--A SLUG!!!
!!
CATCH IT, POP!! I'LL GO GET THE SALT!!
C'MERE, YOU LI'L ♣✖✖♦!!
ZIP
@☆€✖@!!
DIVE
ZOOP
CRUSH
OKAY, POP! I GOT THE SALT!!
SALT
--WHAT HAPPENED?
IT... IT GOT AWAY!!
SALT
SO... AT DINNER...
HURRY UP AN' SAY THE ♣✖✖♦!! GRACE SO WE CAN EAT!
OUR FATHER—FOR WHATEVER THIS IS WE ARE ABOUT TO RECEIVE, MAY YOU... UH... MAY WE BLESS... UH... WELL, THAT IS... WE...
Z
Z
Z
THE END.

© JOE MATT.

29

31

LIFE IN
HELL

IN THE BEGINNING THEY WERE **SMALL** AND **LIGHT**! I HAD FUN THROWING THEM AGAINST THE **WALL**!

NOW LET ME!

NYEEP!

NYEEP!

UNFORTUNATELY, THEY KEPT ON **GROWING** AND LOST SOME OF THEIR **CUTENESS**!

AND I GREW OLDER **MYSELF**!

HONESTLY!

OOPS!

...THEY'RE ALWAYS UNDERFOOT!

NYEEP?

NYEEP!

I BEGAN FINDING MY NANCIES **TEDIOUS** TO HAVE **AROUND**! (MY FOLKS HAD **NEVER** BEEN TOO ENTHRALLED WITH THEM!)

MY **DAD** HEARD ABOUT AN OUTFIT THAT PAID A **COUPLE** OF **BUCKS** APIECE FOR **USED NANCIES**! I DIDN'T **PROTEST** TOO MUCH WHEN HE SUGGESTED THAT PERHAPS THE TIME HAD COME TO **PART COMPANY** WITH THEM!

NYEEP!

NYEEP!

NYEEP!

NYEEP!

HERE Y'ARE, SONNY!

OBOY!

ACME USED NANCY COLLECTION SERVICE

MOBILE NANCY DUMP

I USED THE **MONEY** TO BUY SOME GOOD **COMIC BOOKS** THAT I STILL ENJOY READING **TODAY**!

AN **EXCELLENT** PEN LINE...**CONTROLLED** YET EXPRESSIVE OF THE ETERNAL **AMBIGUITIES** OF **CHILDHOOD**...

Little Lulu

WHAT A **PLEASURE** IT WAS TO WAKE UP TO A WORLD THAT DIDN'T SMELL LIKE **AMMONIA**!

HOWEVER, IT'S A PLEASURE THAT DOESN'T FEEL SO **GOOD** SINCE I'VE LEARNED WHAT **FATE** AWAITS HAPLESS NANCIES WHO GET SENT BACK HOME TO THE **NANCY FARMS** BY COMPLIANT **DUPES** LIKE **ME**!

35

MATURE NANCIES ARE **JAMMED** BY THE **HUNDREDS** INTO HORRIFYING **NANCY BINS**, CREATING SUCH A **STENCH** THAT THEIR **FEEDERS** MUST WEAR **GAS MASKS** TO **APPROACH** THEM!

POOR NUTRITION CAUSES DISFIGURING **WRINKLES** TO COVER THEIR ONCE-LOVABLE **FACES**!

NYEEP!...

NYEEP...

...AND THE **STRESS** OF **OVERCROWDING** RESULTS IN **BIZARRE NEUROTIC BEHAVIOR**—SUCH AS THE MINDLESS **BASHING** OF THEIR **HEADS** TOGETHER FOR HOURS ON END!

SNARL!

BONK!

BONK!

BONK!

HISSS...

VOMIT!

OCCASIONALLY ONE OF THE NANCIES WILL **LEAP** DESPERATELY OVER THE **FENCE** AND MAKE A PATHETIC **DASH** FOR **FREEDOM!**

NYEEP?
NYEEP!
NYEEP!
NYEEP?
NYEEP!

THE **ECONOMICS** OF THE **INDUSTRY** ARE SUCH THAT IT IS MORE COST-EFFICIENT TO **SHOOT** SUCH FUGITIVES ON THE **SPOT** THAN IT WOULD BE TO TRY AND EFFECT A **RE·CAPTURE!**

YEEK!
Cough! Choke!
BLAM!

THE SIGHT OF THE ERRANT NANCY'S **CARCASS** BEING LANGUIDLY **CONSUMED** BY PASSING **SCAVENGERS** SERVES TO **DETER** NANCIES OF SIMILAR **INCLINATION** FROM PUTTING THEIR **ESCAPE FANTASIES** INTO **ACTION!**

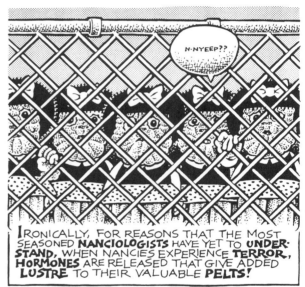

N-NYEEP??

IRONICALLY, FOR REASONS THAT THE MOST SEASONED **NANCIOLOGISTS** HAVE YET TO **UNDER·STAND**, WHEN NANCIES EXPERIENCE **TERROR, HORMONES** ARE RELEASED THAT GIVE ADDED **LUSTRE** TO THEIR VALUABLE **PELTS!**

STILL, I CONFESS THAT I'M **HAUNTED** TO THIS **DAY** BY THE MEMORY OF MY **OWN** SWEET, STINKY NANCIES BEING CARTED DOWN THE **STREET** SO MANY YEARS AGO...

...AND I CAN'T HELP WONDERING...

NYEEP!
NYEEP!
NYEEP!
NYEEP!
NYEEP!
NYEEP!

MOBILE NANCY DUMP

...IS IT **WORTH** IT?

...IS IT **WORTH** THE **AGONY,** MR. & MRS. **FASHION·CONSCIOUS AMERICA?**

OH, HARVEY...

HAPPY ANNIVERSARY, DARLING!

YOU SHOULDN'T HAVE!

CRUSE

the end

39

THIS cave interior is filled with a huge painting, a magical snake symbol being created here by warrior PRIMITIF, using his bare hands. Earthenware jars filled with coloured pigments surround him.

But one look at the snake's head shows he has left gaps for where the eyes should be.

Each IDOL in the village has a specific function. Here, PRIMITIF questions VIRAILLE, God of sight. "Why did you make me paint this serpent?"

"Now my sight is nearly asleep. My eyes are like two dead men."

One day, PRIMITIF, you shall ascend to the warrior's Heaven on condor's wings. There your eyes will become as your hands, and control all that you see.

PRIMITIF is confused and weary. "Was the God speaking to me then?" he thinks. "I must rest. I cannot be more miserable."

But misery seems infinite. Next day, he wakes up totally blind.

In three night's time the entire Village is illuminated by a Bright Whirlwind of fire dancing out of PRIMITIF's hut. All are mystified.

Whisked away to the Desert, the magic Flame disappears behind the Dunes.

"Where's PRIMITIF?" everyone asks. There's his mask Left Behind on the WALL.

Their CONCERN spreads. Sightless, their Bravest warrior may be in Danger. So they search all night.

Located, the errant Hunter is carried back on a stretcher. He is nearly paralyzed.

"We found him in the desert staring transfixed at the moon," they explain to the Medicine Man.

Is his sight Restored? Hard to say: His eyes don't respond to the torch flame.

And yet he describes extraordinary sights he's seen in the DesErt.

Three months go by. VIRAILLE looks down from Heaven, well pleased with his work. But there remains one act of INTERVENTION for him to perform. | Hence the appearance of this Gigantic Snake in the jungle, which encircles PRIMITIF's village.

No man can enter or exit. If PRIMITIF could only see, he being the strongest could easily despatch this serpent. | In despair, everyone retreats to their homes — so nobody sees the Snake of fire coiling out of PRIMITIF's hut. | Next day the warrior stands tall in the clearing, his sight obviously restored.

A circle of bones arrayed around the walls is all that remains of the serpent. But where is the monster's head? | PRIMITIF has cut it off and proudly displays it mounted on a tall sharp stick. Its eyes have been gouged out.

FROM NOW ON PRIMITIF will be forever grateful for the precious gift of SIGHT. He delights in all he sees. | He completes his work by painting a pair of eyes for his snake; and decorates the rest of the cave with his desert visions. | The rest of the tribe are amazed. What can he see that they are all blind to?

written and drawn by ED PINSENT

THE TWIDDLERS

TRANSLATED BY: ELIZABETH BELL   LETTERED BY: LEA HERNANDEZ

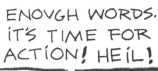

ENOUGH WORDS. IT'S TIME FOR ACTION! HEIL!

NO SOONER SAID THAN DONE: AN ARMY OF NAZIDIDDLES TROOPS OFF.

INEVITABLY, THE HAIR-RAISING ENCOUNTER OCCURS, AND WITH THIRTY AGAINST THREE OUR FRIENDS DON'T HAVE THE GHOST OF A CHANCE.

HA! HA! THERE'S ONE, WITH A COUPLE OF BUDDIES! ATTACK!

YEOW! THE NAZIDIDDLES.

GRR.

FRIENDS, I THINK THIS MEANS TROUBLE!

49

NATURALLY, THEY'RE OFF LIKE A SHOT, THE NAZIDIDDLES HARD ON THEIR HEELS. AT THIS SPEED, THEY CAN'T LAST!

IT'S TOO MUCH!

GLUB

WILL OUR THREE TWIDDLERS WRIGGLE OUT OF THIS ONE? IF THE NAZIDIDDLES GET THEIR "HANDS" ON THEM, THEY'LL DEFINITELY BE TORTURED !!!

PLUS VITE.

DAS TORTURES

OH NON!

51

1.

53

3.

END 4.

© 1990 JIM WOODRING

BUSTER IN MOUTH CITY.......

POIT!

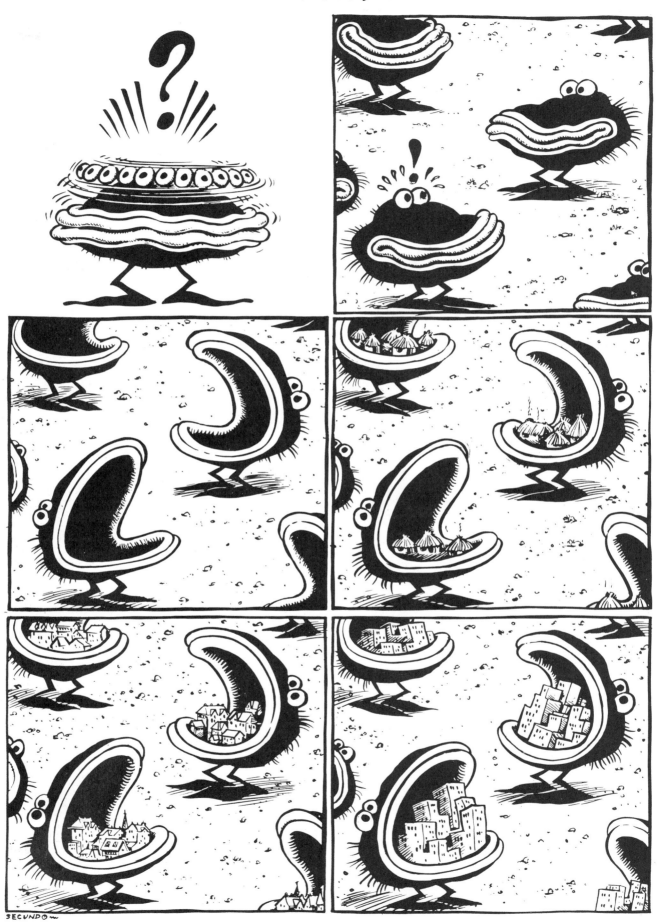

56

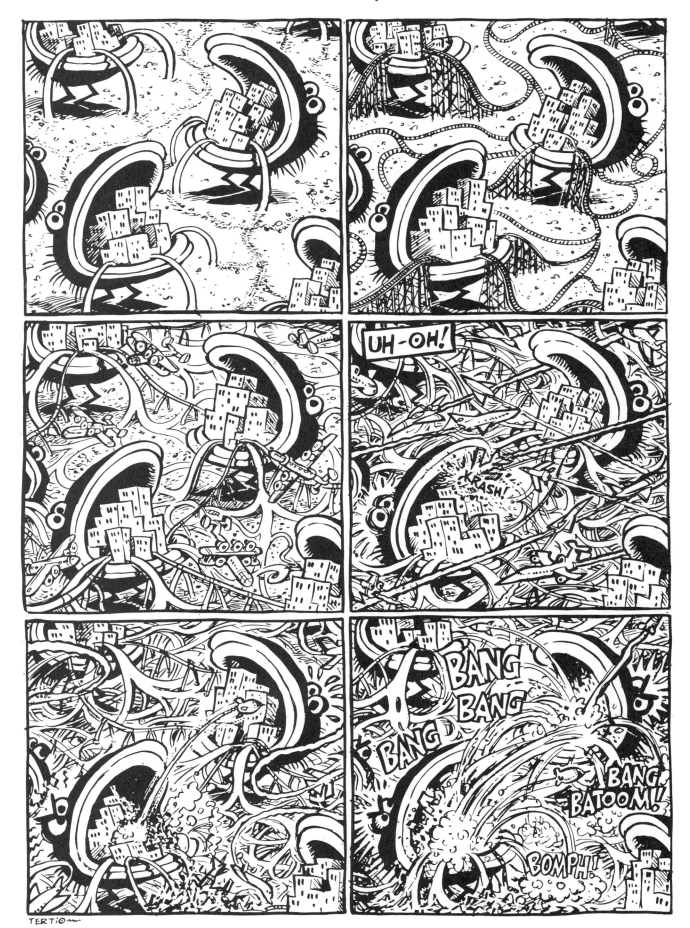

FAREWELL TO CHARLIE CHAPLIN

RICK GEARY ©1981

JUST THIS YEAR I MOVE TO SWITZERLAND WITH MY CLOSE FRIEND SVOD

WE LOOK ALL OVER FOR WORK

MY WIFE AND MY INFANT ARE HERE TOO

WE ALL OCCUPY A ROOM IN THIS HOUSE

A CORNER OF OUR ROOM

MY NEIGHBOR FROM THE ROOM NEXT DOOR SAYS THAT THE PICTURE STAR CHARLIE CHAPLIN IS BURIED AT A VILLAGE NEAR US

ONE NIGHT MY NEIGHBOR AND MY FRIEND AND ME DIG UP MR. CHAPLIN

WE MUST PUSH HIS COFFIN ALONG THE GROUND

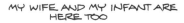

59

THE HOLE WE LEAVE

WE HIDE MR. CHAPLIN IN THE CELLAR OF OUR HOUSE

TO BE SAFE, WE BURN OUR CLOTHES AND SHOES

WE DROP OUR SHOVELS INTO THE RIVER

MY FRIEND TELEPHONES A RANSOM DEMAND FROM A CABINET IN THE CENTRE OF TOWN

I ADMIRE THE FINE OAKWORK AND FITTINGS OF MR. CHAPLIN'S COFFIN

WE WATCH ABOUT OUR CRIME ON MY NEIGHBOR'S TELEVISION

MEANTIME I WORK IN THE AUTO GARAGE TO SUPPORT MY FAMILY

MY FRIEND CONTINUES TO TELEPHONE RANSOM DEMANDS

MY NEIGHBOR IS UPSET AND
SAYS THAT WE HAD BETTER
GET OUR MONEY SOON

MY WIFE WANTS MR. CHAPLIN
REMOVED FROM THE HOUSE

MY NEIGHBOR AND MY FRIEND
AND ME, REMOVE MR. CHAPLIN
TO A PASTURE FAR AWAY

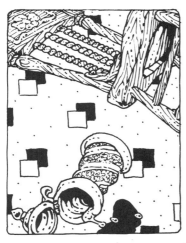

AFTER CONSIDERABLE DISCUSSION
WE DECIDE TO LOWER OUR
RANSOM DEMAND

MY NEIGHBOR LEAVES TO
VISIT HIS COUSIN IN BERN

MY FRIEND IS PLACED UNDER
ARREST AS HE TELEPHONES
ANOTHER RANSOM DEMAND

WE MUST SHOW WHERE TO
FIND MR. CHAPLIN

MY WIFE AND MY INFANT MUST
RETURN TO BULGARIA

MY FRIEND AND ME IN THE
CUSTODY OF THE GOVERNMENT

61

62

hello, friend farmer! i've come to end my life here in your field! i hope you received my letter. did you?

No? No matter, this'll only take a second...excuse me, i'm a bit out of breath, i just arrived from Paris...

...ahh, Paris! been there? deep down, i adore Paris...i could never really leave... ...and yet these huge cities have become unlivable!...if you knew how i'd love to end my days in the country!

...but how can i reconcile that goal with my unswerving affection for Paris? Eh? twist the problem any which way, there's only one solution: to throw myself off the Eiffel tower into a country field! i just brought along a few beams of it, enough for my purpose...

TRANSLATION BY: ELIZABETH BELL   LETTERING BY: LEA HERNANDEZ

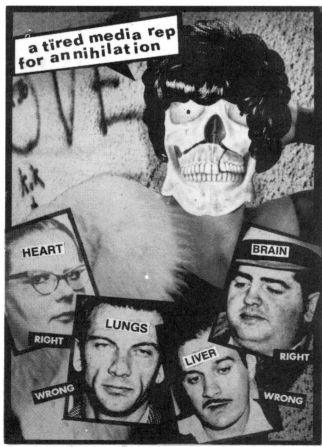

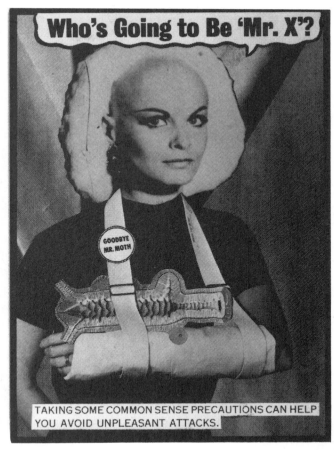

68

robert sikoryak

Believe It Or Else!

JOHN CAGE

American Avant-Garde Composer (b. 1912) HAS BEEN WRITING ANECDOTES ABOUT HIS LIFE FOR MANY YEARS — WHEN READ IN A RANDOM ORDER, THEY ARE MEANT TO ILLUSTRATE THE WAY IN WHICH ALL THINGS— PEOPLE, EVENTS, AND PLACES — ARE RELATED

THE PREPARED PIANO HAS RUBBER BANDS, WOODEN SPOONS, BITS OF METAL, AND PAPER JAMMED BETWEEN ITS STRINGS TO PRODUCE UNUSUAL SOUNDS Submitted by J. Cage of New York, N.Y.

THE SKUNK CABBAGE, an edible mushroom, IS VIRTUALLY IDENTICAL TO THE POISONOUS HELLEBORE, BUT LOOKS NOTHING LIKE THE EDIBLE FIELD MUSHROOM

he tried a club.
This defense le
desired. Declarer w
his high spades. W,
didn't drop, he led
finesse with dumm
threw a heart on th
monds. He lost onl
diamond and a heart.

HEART CAN'T

East was beside him
have to lead a heart," he
"I can see that now,"
sourly. "But what if you c
the ace of hearts?"
"What if I didn't?"
back. "The man's bidd
nine black cards. If he
hearts, he could disc
heart on a diamond ev
an old shoe. Lead
couldn't cost, and if I
we'd have to grab ou
right awa

JUNE 5, 1988

NEW YORK, N.Y.

Indeterminacy
THE COMICS SUPPLEMENT

Quick Concerto

John and Henry

FATHER PAUL

Kitty Kook

BROWNIE

SUZUKI, ZEN MASTER

Our Story: MASTER SUZUKI HAS TRAVELLED FAR FROM THE EAST TO SPEAK OF HIS PHILOSOPHY. MANY HAVE GATHERED TO LISTEN, INCLUDING JON.

THE MASTER SPEAKS SOFTLY. THE BUSTLE OUTSIDE HIS WINDOW DROWNS OUT HIS WORDS; HE DOES NOT REPEAT HIMSELF.

JON STRUGGLES TO HEAR, YET HE CANNOT FATHOM ANYTHING THAT IS BEING SAID.

BUT A WEEK LATER, WHILE WALKING THROUGH THE WOODS, IT ALL DAWNS ON HIM.

NEXT – Enlightenment

They'll Do Windows

HOUSEWORK BRINGS OUT THE ROMANTIC IN AUNT MARGE—

YOU KNOW, I LOVE THIS MACHINE MUCH MORE THAN I DO YOUR UNCLE WALTER!

Thanx to "SILENCE"
©1967 JOHN CAGE
WESLEYAN U. PRESS

THE MAD AD MAN

GENTLEMEN, MEET JOHN CAGE, THE COMPOSER— HE'S WILLING TO PROSTITUTE HIS ART FOR OUR RADIO ADS

CALL IN THE STAFF – I WANT THEM TO HEAR JOHN'S MUSIC

DIFFERENT! INCREDIBLE! NUTTY! NEW! AMAZING! IMPROVED!

YOU'RE TOO GOOD FOR US—WE'RE SAVING YOU FOR ROBINSON CRUSOE!

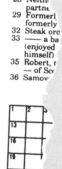

Little Guys

WHAT DID YOU THINK OF TODAY'S CONCERT?

OH, I ENJOYED THE MUSIC...

BUT I DIDN'T AGREE WITH THE PROGRAM NOTE ABOUT THERE BEING TOO MUCH PAIN IN THE WORLD...

WHAT? YOU DON'T THINK THERE'S ENOUGH?

NO, I THINK THERE'S JUST THE RIGHT AMOUNT!

75

FAMOUS Frauds

NO. 1. IN A SERIES
THE ADVENTURES OF DON CARLOS BALMORI
A TRUE STORY

"NOTHING IS AS IT APPEARS TO BE, NOT EVEN I!"

OUR STORY OPENS IN **MEXICO CITY**. THE YEAR IS **1927**, AND WE FIND OURSELVES AT A PARTY WITH THE CREAM OF MEXICAN SOCIETY.

AMONG THE GUESTS IS **CARLOS GONZALES**, A RISING REAL ESTATE BROKER.

SEÑOR DON CARLOS BALMORI

INTRODUCING **DON CARLOS BALMORI**, RUMORED TO BE THE RICHEST MAN IN **MEXICO**!

SEÑOR GONZALES, I HAVE HEARD OF YOUR GREAT PROWESS AS A SALESMAN.

YOU FLATTER ME SEÑOR!

YOU KNOW SEÑOR, I WOULD CONSIDER IT A GREAT FORTUNE TO HAVE A MAN OF YOUR CALIBRE WORKING FOR ME.

PERHAPS YOU MIGHT CONSIDER AN ANNUAL RETAINER OF SAY $500,000.00, OVER AND ABOVE YOUR COMMISSIONS OF COURSE.

SEÑOR, I AM SO HAPPY I DO NOT KNOW WHAT TO SAY, I, I,.....

THERE IS **ONE** PROVISION HOWEVER THAT I **MUST** INSIST UPON.

CALL IT AN ECCENTRICITY IF YOU WILL BUT I INSIST THAT ALL WHO WORK FOR ME MUST BE CLEAN SHAVEN.

BUT **SEÑOR!** EVEN MY WIFE HAS NEVER SEEN ME WITHOUT MY BEARD!

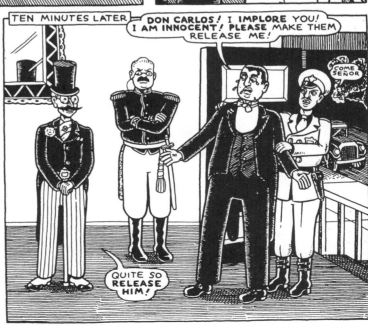

AND WITH THAT...

WHY, WHY,..... YOU ARE A **WOMAN**!!

SEÑOR, ALLOW ME TO INTRODUCE SEÑORITA CONCEPCIÓN JURADO

WHAT DOES THIS MEAN?

I WILL TRY TO EXPLAIN...

YOU SEE **SEÑOR**, **EVERYONE** IN THIS ROOM HAS AT ONE TIME OR ANOTHER, BEEN A **VICTIM** OF THE **NON EXISTENT DON CARLOS**, JUST AS **YOU** WERE TONIGHT.

I MYSELF WAS TRICKED INTO APPEARING NAKED AT A SPECIAL NEW YEAR'S EVE MASQUERADE PARTY. IT WAS PROMISED THAT MY IDENTITY WOULD BE CONCEALED BUT,....

COME **SEÑOR**, IT IS **MIDNIGHT**! TIME FOR EVERYONE TO **UNMASK**!

BONG BONG BONG

BUT (CHUCKLE) HOW COME I DID NOT HEAR OF IT?

BECAUSE **SEÑOR**, LIKE THE OTHERS, YOU WILL BE SWORN TO **SECRECY**!

THAT IS OF COURSE IF YOU WANT NO WORD OF TONIGHT'S TRAVESTY TO **LEAK OUT**!

PHONY STICK PIN

VICTIMS IN THE NEWSPAPER GAME, HELPED FAN THE FLAMES OF THIS **BIZARRE HOAX**, BY PUBLISHING AN ENDLESS STREAM OF **FAKED** PHOTOS. THESE PICTURES PURPORTED TO SHOW THE GREAT "MAN" WITH FAMOUS CELEBRITIES, OFF ON EXOTIC HUNTS, AND PERFORMING THE VARIOUS DUTIES THAT ARE EXPECTED OF A PUBLIC FIGURE.

SEEN HERE IN 1928 WITH U.S. STARS RUDY VALLEE AND LARRY FARREL

THUS **CARLOS GONZALES** JOINED THE SECRET ARMY OF **PROMINENT MEXICANS** THAT KEPT THE MYTH OF **DON CARLOS BALMORI** ALIVE!

MR. SAN ANTONIO

IN PRIVATE **SEÑORITA JURADO** LED A CHASTE AND PIOUS EXISTENCE;

BUT OF COURSE IT WAS AS **DON CARLOS** THAT SHE **REALLY** LIVED!

AND **DON CARLOS** WAS FOREVER BEING LINKED ROMANTIC-ALLY WITH THE CHOICEST PLUMS IN MEXICO'S SOCIAL REGISTER.

DON CARLOS, ALLOW ME TO PRESENT MY NIECE

MAJOR! WHERE HAVE YOU BEEN HIDING **THIS** ONE!

ONE EVENING **DON CARLOS** WAS INTRODUCED TO **SEÑORITA MARÍA ANTONIETA**

THE EVENING PROGRESSED RAPIDLY,...

....TO AN **UNEXPECTED** CLIMAX.

THIS MINOR SETBACK NOTWITHSTANDING, THE **BALMORI** LEGEND REMAINED INTACT.

WHEN DEATH CAME IN **1931**, THE BAN ON HER SECRET WAS LIFTED.

TODAY THE SURVIVORS OF THIS BIZARRE HOAX MAKE AN ANNUAL PILGRIMAGE TO HER SHRINE. HERE ON THE OUTSKIRTS OF **MEXICO CITY**, THEY PAY HOMAGE TO THIS BELOVED RASCAL OF YORE.

Kim Deitch -75

79

THOSE IRREPRESSIBLE FUNSTERS...

MORE LAUGH MAKERS

BY DREW FRIEDMAN

"UGLIEST MAN IN HOLLYWOOD," SHEMP HOWARD HAD HIS PICK AMONGST A VIRTUAL SMORGASBORD OF TINSELTOWN STARLETS.

HEE BEE BEE BEE BEE BEE BEE BEE BEE BEE...

KNOWN AS A MAN OF FEW WORDS, WALLY COX POURED OUT HIS SOUL SHORTLY BEFORE HIS UNTIMELY DEATH.

WELL, IF IT'S A TOSS UP BETWEEN PEEPERS AND UNDERDOG, I'D HAVE TO GO WITH THE DOG AS MY PREFERENCE.

EVEN THOUGH THE JOBS WERE NO MORE FOR RICHARD DEACON, HE CONTINUED TO HANG AROUND THE STUDIOS ANYWAY.

WHAT TH' HELL'S HE DOIN' HERE?

I DUNNO. HE'S RICHARD DEACON.

EDGAR BUCHANAN WAS DISGRUNTLED OVER THE COURSE FILMMAKING TOOK IN THE EARLY SEVENTIES.

NO, SIR. IT JUST AIN'T LIKE THOSE OLD DAYS.

WACKY HEE HAW STAR JUNIOR SAMPLES WOULD ROUND UP THE NEIGHBORHOOD CHILDREN FOR BIRTHDAY PARTIES ON ANY GIVEN DAY.

WE'RE GONNA HAVE SOME FUN. HAH!

TOWARD THE END OF HIS EXISTENCE, JOE E. ROSS BROUGHT HIS DATES TO FOREST LAWN FOR "WOOPIE."

OOH...OOH... GIMME A LITTLE SMOOCH, DOLL. I'M A CELEBRITY.

END

drew freidman

LAUGH MAKERS

BY DREW FREIDMAN

©1981

BUD ABBOTT MADE HIS FINAL STAGE APPEARANCE IN 1974 AT THE OLD ACTORS HOME IN LOS ANGELES. HE WAS DEAD A WEEK LATER.

COSTELLA...

CLAP! CLAP! CLAP! CLAP! CLAP! CLAP! CLAP!

WHEN MOE HOWARD & LARRY FINE DIED IN 1974, JOE DiRITA WAS LEFT OUT IN THE COLD.

SHORTLY BEFORE HIS FATAL STROKE IN 1957, OLIVER HARDY WOULD TAKE LONG WALKS IN THE PARK, DRESSED ONLY IN HIS WIFE'S FROCK.

MY, IT'S A LOVELY DAY, IS'NT IT, MR. FINLAYSON?

MR. FINLAYSON

FORMER MGM CARTOON PRODUCER FRED QUIMBY CONTEMPLATES ART SPIEGELMAN'S "MAUS."

81

DOODLES WEAVER, FORMER MEMBER OF SPIKE JONES ZANY BAND, ENJOYS STROLLING THROUGH URBAN GETTOS. THE BELOVED FUNNYMAN IS CURRENTLY UNDER HOSPITAL CARE FOR SEVERE HEAD CONCUSSIONS. SHOULD RECOVER SOON.

IN 1979, JIMMY NELSON BURIED DANNY O'DAY & FARFEL.

NESTLE MAKES THE VERY BEST...

CHOCOLATE?

TO BE CONTINUED

LAUGH MAKERS

Second of a Series

BY DREW FRIEDMAN

ARTHUR Q. BRYAN, VOICE OF ELMER FUDD, SPENT HIS LAST DAYS SITTING ON HIS STAIRS.

WABBITS!!

MANTAN MORELAND ENJOYS THE GOOD LIFE.

WHO DAT?

STAR OF PETE SMITH SHORTS DAVE O'BRIEN NOW TALKS TO BIRDS.

PETE SMITH IS DEAD!

& FISH

MOUSIE GARNER DELIVERS HIS OWN ELEGY.

I PAID MY DUES... 'S TIME FOR FAME.

IN HIS FINAL DAYS, EL BRENDEL WAS PROUDEST OF HIS KITCHENWARE.

VONCE I MADE A QUARTER MILLION DOLLARS A YEAR. IT'SA VACKY VORLD.

A MASSIVE WEIGHT LOSS HAD DON WILSON THINKING COMEBACK. HE WAS DEAD WITHIN THE MONTH.

I'LL BE BELOVED IN AMERICANS HEARTS ONCE MORE.

WITH JUST HOURS TO LIVE, FRANK FONTAINE DECIDED TO BE FUNNY.

LARRY FINE OFTEN REFERED TO HIS PARALYZING STROKE AS HIS "STROKE OF LUCK."

I LIVE A FULL AND HAPPY LIFE.

THE END

© 1982

82

WALLOWING IN THEIR WACKY DESPAIR...

LAUGH MAKERS

BY DREW FRIEDMAN

IN HIS FINAL YEAR OF LIFE, JACKIE COOGAN WANDERED THROUGH CEMETERIES IN SEARCH OF PAST GLORIES.

IN THE FALL OF '73, JOE E. BROWN FILLED HIS BEVERLY HILLS POOL WITH BOWEL MOVEMENTS.

WOOOW! DOES THIS STINK!

SHORTLY BEFORE HIS DEATH, BERT LAHR'S BEHAVIOR BECAME ERRATIC.

LAY'S POTATO CHIPS...COURAGE... LAY'S POTATO CHIPS... COURAGE...LAY'S POTATO CHIPS...

CARTOON DIRECTOR PAUL J. SMITH SPEAKS OF HIS ERSTWHILE COMPETITION...

YEAH, WELL, FUCK DISNEY AND HIS GODDAMN MOUSE.

THE WPIX-TV YULE LOG IS A BELOVED TRADITION IN THE HOME OF SPORTS-CASTER WARNER WOLF'S FATHER, COMIC SAMMY WOLF.

AFTER HIS RETIREMENT FROM "BEWITCHED," DICK YORK WAS OFTEN SPOTTED IN STRANGE ATTIRE.

YEAH, IT'S ME AND YOU'D BETTER WIPE THAT SMILE OFF YOUR FACE, MAC.

END

art spiegelman

"AS THEY STARTED OUT THE DOOR, GERTRUDE HANDED PICASSO...THE COMICS SECTION FROM ONE OF THE AMERICAN SUNDAY PAPERS: THE PAINTER WAS AN AVID FOLLOWER OF THE KATZENJAMMER KIDS AND OF LITTLE JIMMY. PICASSO BEAMED AND THANKED HER."

Chapter One: THE SHORT GOODBYE!

84

Chapter Two: NO POCKETS IN A MIDGET, DON'T THEY?

88

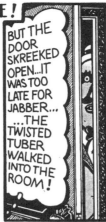

art spiegelman

Chapter Five: ACE DEFECTIVE, MIDGET HOLE.

91

displaying a nihilistic, violent sensibility , the new punk funnies soon became the most provocative and perhaps the most prophetic branch of the entire new comics movement. ugly art was not without precedent in comics history, however. in the 1940s, in the work of basil wolverton, for example, the grotesque was brought to heights it has seldom, if ever, realized since. the artists who represent this branch of the new comics movement are all wolverton's children, whether they know it or not.

the NEW
punk funnies

94 BUMS AND THE BIRD SPIRIT
by S. Clay Wilson

A midwinter's night dream was the source for this rare, two page narrative strip from the Underground master of the greater apocalyptic arts.

96 TERROR FROM THE GRAVE
by Rory Hayes

The levels of inner psychic terror which inhabited the works of the late Rory Hayes grow even more intense as the years go by.

97 THE UNPLEASANT SUBWAY
by Mark Beyer

Urban life continues to be one long, continually unfolding nightmare for Amy Tilsdale and her friend Jordan, in the world's first post-modern comic strip.

99 DUST TO DUST
by Krystine Kryttre

A scratch-board prayer against drug abuse by one of the great cartoonists to emerge from the punk underground of San Francisco.

100 ZOMBIES ON BROADWAY
by Kaz

The rats can be found directly under the New Jersey pavement in this early classic of punk dementia by Hoboken's favorite underground artist.

102 MY ANCESTORS
by Bruce Hilvitz

A lovely tribute to the days of the old Wisconsin Death Trip by the East Bay's most irregular member of the local 4-H club.

103 THE ROBBERY
by Julie Doucet

The great Doucet — formerly of Montreal, currently of New York City — turns the sights of her own fantastic imagination to the liberating flight of petty crime.

105 BUDDHA POPEYE
by Roy Tompkins

An eight-armed junkie realizes his essential dharma-hood while flying upon his skateboard o'er the Land of the Living Dead.

106 THE CRAZY MEN ROLLER COASTER AND TURNPIKE
by Michael Roden

This two page strip might seem unusual to you, but for Ohio's Michael Roden, what's another average Saturday afternoon down at your favorite neighborhood amusement park?

108 THE NEW WORLD
by Pasquito Bolino

One of the younger artists featured in the lunatic *Chemical Imbalance* magazine provide new work just for this anthology.

109 THE JOB
by Y5/P5

The clown prince of Paris's new punk underground writes a special little tale of heartbreak for all his English-language-reading friends.

111 PARFUME DE LA MORT
by Mary Fleener

Picasso meets Jim Thompson in this sweet little murder tale from the neon-lit wonderlands of Southern California.

113 ALL CONSUMING GUILT
by Jim Shaw

L.A. Gallery Artist Jim Shaw satirizes the comic strip offerings of a fascinating, Los Angeles-based, right-wing fundamentalist preacher.

114 BAD
by Maruo Suehiro

The legendary popularity of America's richest modern entertainer is called into question by one of the leaders of Tokyo's punk underground.

116 MR. CRUSE
by Peter Kuper

The author of "Tales of New York" allows how strange it can be waiting for a nightime cab on the streets of old Gotham.

117 SHOWDOWN AT RIO BOBO
by Mack White

Austin's leading gunslinger tells us things were often more bizarre than they seemed in the Old West — particularly in you were a traveling ventriloquist!

119 IT WAS DINOBOY'S FINEST HOUR
by Paul Mavrides

DinoBoy joins the Heavenly Choir in Beetle Heaven — an early outrage from the psychedelic wing of San Francisco's underground punk culture.

120 FUN FESTER DIGESTER
by Jonathon Rosen

Recent body work from the latest genius to emerge from New York City's avant-garde comics underground.

122 WONDERLAND
by Pascal Doury

The laws of kinetics are curved and twisted in the service of magic in the wood-toy wonderland of France's most imaginative New Comics artists.

124 THE JUNKIE
by Bruno Richard

A "signature" illustration from one of the founders of France's burgeoning "gangster art" new punk underground.

125 THE ROUSTABOUT
by Gary Panter

Ultimately the wild beauty of the language carries this tribute by the "Father of Punk Comics" to the greatest Weirdo King of this century.

THE BUMS WERE STANDING AROUND.. KILLING TIME. THEMSELVES.. BELCHING. SCRATCHING. FARTING. PUKING. PASSING THE JUG. PASSING OUT..

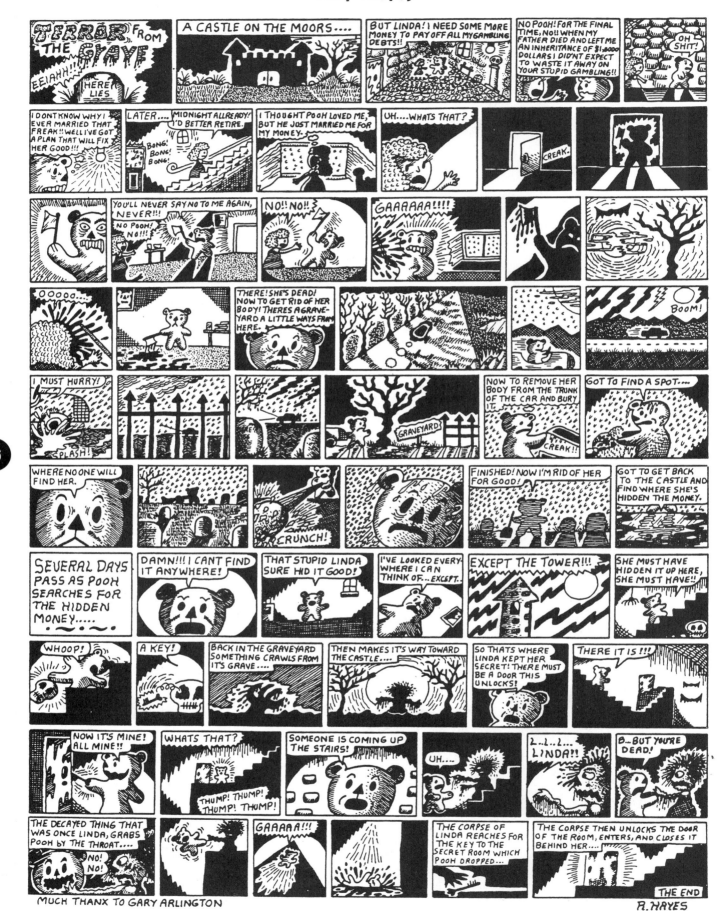

MUCH THANX TO GARY ARLINGTON

R. HAYES

DUST TO DUST

© 1985 KRYSTINE KRYTTRE

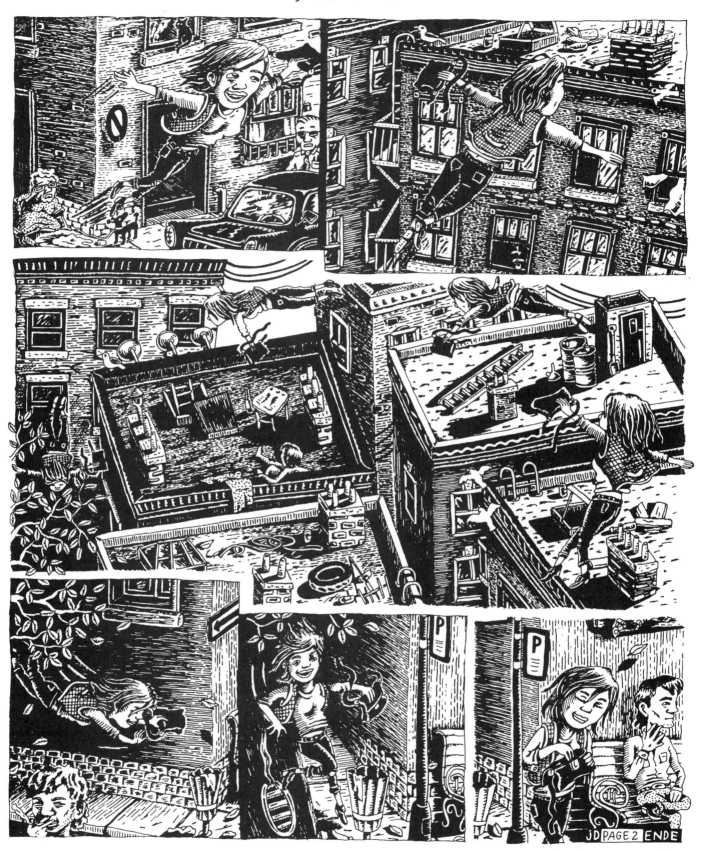

the J.OB

110

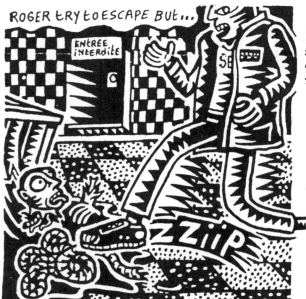

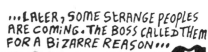

APROXIMATIVE ENGLISH, ISNT IT?

PARFUME de la MORT

© M. FLEENER '87

SHE WAS PUTTING ON HER MAKE-UP WHEN SHE FIRST NOTICED THE SMELL.

IT DIDN'T SEEM TO BE IN ONE PLACE, SO SHE WENT TO WORK AND FORGOT ABOUT IT.

THE NEXT DAY SHE WAS MAKING BREAKFAST WHEN SHE SMELLED IT AGAIN

"TIME TO DO THESE DISHES."

111

STILL THE SMELL REMAINED SO SHE WASHED, VACUUMED, SCRUBBED, WAXED, AND OPENED ALL THE WINDOWS

IT DIDN'T HELP

THE NEXT SEVERAL DAYS BECAME A BATTLE BETWEEN HER NOSE AND HER BRAIN. SLEEP WAS IMPOSSIBLE...

HER CLOTHES BEGAN TO TAKE ON THE STENCH, THE FOOD SHE ATE TASTED BAD AND SHE BEGAN TO GO A LITTLE CRAZY.

SUNDAY MORNING THE LANDLADY CAME TO COLLECT RENT AS SHE ALWAYS DID AT THE END OF THE MONTH

 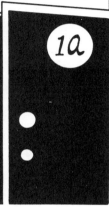

THE OLD WOMAN WENT TO THE DOWNSTAIRS APARTMENT AND KNOCKED ON THE DOOR. IT WAS UNLOCKED AND OPEN.

THE HUSBAND SHOT HIS WIFE WHO WAS SITTING ON THE COUCH

AND HE WAS FACING HER HOLDING THE GUN THAT HE HAD SHOT HIMSELF WITH.

THE POLICE CAME AND GUESSED THEY'D BEEN DEAD FOR THREE WEEKS

OF COURSE, THERE WAS A NOTE

THAT NIGHT, THE GIRL UPSTAIRS WAS HAPPY. THE SMELL WAS GONE.

based on a true incident; Hermosa Beach, Calif., 1977

ALL CONSUMING GUILT

OH MAN!! I GOT THE MUNCHIES REAL BAD! I GOTTA GET SOME SNACKFOOD REAL FAST!

RIGHT ON, MAN!!

SOME BEER AND SOME YO-GURT AND SOME SCREAMING YELLOW ZONKERS AND SOME FRITOS AND...

EXCUSE ME.

HUH?!?

YOUNG MAN, DID YOU KNOW THAT EVERY TIME YOU TAKE A BITE OUT OF SIN, GUILT TAKES A BITE OUT OF YOU?

WHAT ARE YOU, A NARC OR SOME THIN'?

NO, I HAVE ACCEPTED JESUS CHRIST AS MY PERSONAL SAVIOR.

SO YOU'RE A RELIGIOUS FANATIC?

YES, AND I'M GOING TO TRY AND SAVE YOUR SOUL.

BUT MAN, I DON'T HAVE A SOUL. I'M ONLY FLESH & BLOOD.

WHY DO YOU THINK YOU WERE PUT HERE ON EARTH, TO EAT JUNK FOOD TILL YOU DIE OF A HEART ATTACK? THEN YOUR SOUL & FAT WILL BURN ON THE BRAZIERS OF HELL FOR ALL ETERNITY!

OH WOW! WHY DIDN'T ANYONE TELL ME THIS BEFORE?

BECAUSE THE MAJOR FOOD CORPORATIONS ARE CONJOINED IN A CONSPIRACY TO SEND AS MANY SOULS TO HELL AS POSSIBLE!!

HOW WILL THEY DO THAT?!

BY FEEDING YOU FOOD THAT IS IMPRINTED WITH THE MARK OF SATAN, LIKE THOSE RITZ CRACKERS OVER THERE AND THAT CRESCENT MOON SYMBOL ON SOAP PACKAGES.

GEE, I NEVER SAW THAT BEFORE!!

OF COURSE NOT!

EVEN ROMAN CATHOLIC COMMUNION WAFERS HAVE SATANIC SYMBOLS PRINTED ON THEM!!

EAT OF MY FLESH

IT'S REALLY ONLY A CONTINUATION OF THE PAGAN CUSTOM OF CANNABALISING THE DEAD TO ASSUME THEIR POWERS. NEVER EAT SACRAMENTS!!!

NEW! TREAT!!

BUT WHAT ABOUT THIS YOGURT? SURELY THERE'S NOTHING PRINTED ON IT!

FOOD DOES NOT NEED SYMBOLS EMBEDDED TO BE SINFUL!

GUILT

WHEN ADAM AND EVE ATE OF THE FOOD OF THE TREE OF KNOWLEDGE THEY COMMITED ORIGINAL SIN AND THEIR FLESH MADE BRUTISH. WHEN THEY ACQUIRED DIGESTIVE TRACTS THEY KNEW THEY WERE BANISHED FOREVER FROM THE GARDEN OF EDEN!!

ALL THAT WE EAT TODAY CONTINUES TO MAKE US BRUTISH AND WE EMIT FOUL SMELLS AS BAD AS THE STINK OF HELL-FIRE!!

BURP

YOU MUST ONLY PARTAKE OF THE FOOD YOU NEED FOR SUSTENANCE, JUST AS YOU MAY ONLY HAVE CARNAL KNOWLEDGE SO THAT YOU MAY REPRODUCE.!!

SNAP!

YES, REMEMBER " IT IS EASIER FOR A FAT MAN TO GO THROUGH THE EYE OF A NEEDLE THAN TO PASS THROUGH THE GATES OF HEAVEN"

YOUR NAME DOES NOT APPEAR IN THE BOOK OF LIFE.

HOW CAN I SAVE MY OWN SOUL? WHAT DO I DO?

GET OUT YOUR BIBLE AND START FASTING AND PRAYING AS ADAM DID TO ATONE FOR HIS SIN, REGAIN HIS BETTER NATURE AND RE-ENTER EDEN.

NOW WAIT JUST A MINUTE PAL! DON'T START COSTING ME SALES! I'M A BUSINESSMAN!

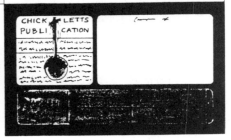

HERE KID, HAVE THIS CANDY BAR AND DON'T FORGET THIS MEDALION.

DON'T LISTEN TO THAT WIERDO. HE'S A FLAKE WHO'S ALWAYS DRIVIN' AWAY THE CUSTOMERS

UH, GOSH THANKS

CHOKE!

CRASH!

OKAY KID, YOU'VE GOT TO KEEP EATING THOSE THREE MUSKETEERS BARS FOREVER!!!

OH WOW, MAN WHAT A BUMMER!!

CHICK PUBLICATION

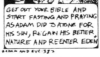

113

TRANSLATED BY: HIROSHI AMANO
LETTERED BY: LEA HERNANDEZ

115

SHOWDOWN AT RIO BOBO BY MACK WHITE

IT WAS A HOT DUSTY AFTERNOON WHEN THE **STRANGER** CAME TO TOWN.

HOWDY, I'M **CHUCK CARSON**, VENTRILOQUIST COWBOY, AND THIS IS MY LITTLE SADDLE PAL, **BOY HOWDY!** GIMME' A SHOT OF **MILK**, BARKEEP!

"MILK." HEH-HEH!

IF IT'S **MOTHER'S MILK** YOU WANT, I SEEN A **MANGY BITCH** OUT BACK LOOKS LIKE SHE MIGHT BE A **RELATION** A' YOUR'N!

YEAH, AND THAT **RAT CARCASS** SHE'S CHEWIN' ON LOOKS LIKE **YOUR** MOTHER!

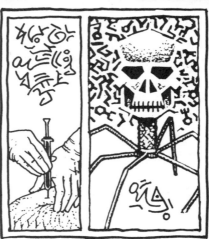

PAUL MAVRIDES

gary panter

THE MELANCHOLY ROUSTABOUT

The anesthetized alien visits men's hell. Inside it's dark and cool. That backside of the hill, however, is no laughing matter.

125

Henry! Nightly! Screaming resurrections of fire with love for you Martyred, sacrificed, consumed.

The melancholy roustabout was out tasting the Longhorn community air. He's wild at the county fair. On the spring-load arm-chair revolvers lights hotrod steel-wool fuses Bright shelling eyeburn.

Charlie don't want out—has real nightmares of a decomposed Elvis Fright-wave collaring the creature out of him. He's afraid of the new worse family He wants no excuse but good.

127

Elvis powers through the imagination of a 16 year-old Mexican baby-sitter; as strange in Death as in life. Elvis fries down the door.

Living Color

Living coLor the artists chosen for this section of the new comics anthology reflect the widest possible range of culture promptings and concerns. viewed in the glow of these lights, lynda barry's "jimmy rodgers," and robert williams' "Hot rod tales" belong as much to a tradition of american "folk art" — from olof krans and john kane to morris hirshfield and ralph fasanella — as they do to the world of comics. the best color art of richard sala and charles burns celebrates contemporary popular culture, where the world has now become cynical, cosmopolitan, and self-conscious in tone. and yet, nothing in the american experience can quite prepare the viewer, for the sensual beauty, the sense of elan, and yes, the smudged hand of decadence, found in the color art of italy's Lorenzo mattotti and france's jacques Loustal. in the end, it is david sandlin's folk jesus figure alone who speaks out for transcendence.

Jimmie Rodgers
1897 – 1933

JIMMIE RODGERS WAS BORN IN MERIDIAN, MISSIS-SIPPI HIS MOTHER DIED WHEN HE WAS FIVE AND HE HAD A HARD BUT INTERESTING CHILDHOOD FOL-LOWING HIS FATHER, A RAILROAD FOREMAN, THROUGH DIFFERENT CITIES IN THE SOUTH, LIVING ON THE ROAD OR BETWEEN RELATIVES. MANY OF THE RAIL WORKERS WERE BLACK AND JIMMIE SERVED AS THEIR WATER BOY AND LEARNED THE MUSIC THEY SANG. AT 13 HE JOINED A MEDICINE SHOW AND TRAVELED AROUND ONLY TO RETURN TO WORK THE RAILS HIMSELF. IN 1927 HE PUT TOGETHER TWO STYLES OF MUSIC THAT WOULD FATHER COUNTRY WESTERN MUSIC AS WE KNOW IT TODAY: BLUES AND YODELING. HE BECAME A BIG SUCCESS WITH HIS MOURNFUL SONGS ABOUT HARD TIMES, TRAINS AND LOST LOVE, AND BEGAN TO TOUR ALL OVER. HE WAS STRICKEN WITH TUBERCULOSIS BUT COULD NOT BEAR TO REST LONG ENOUGH TO RECOVER. HIS HEALTH BECAME INCREASINGLY FRAIL AND AGAINST DOCTOR'S ORDERS HE TRAVELED TO NEW YORK TO A RECORDING SES-SION. HE WAS SO WEAK HE HAD TO LAY ON A COT BETWEEN SESSIONS. HE DIED A COUPLE OF DAYS LATER IN A ROOM AT THE TAFT HOTEL.

134

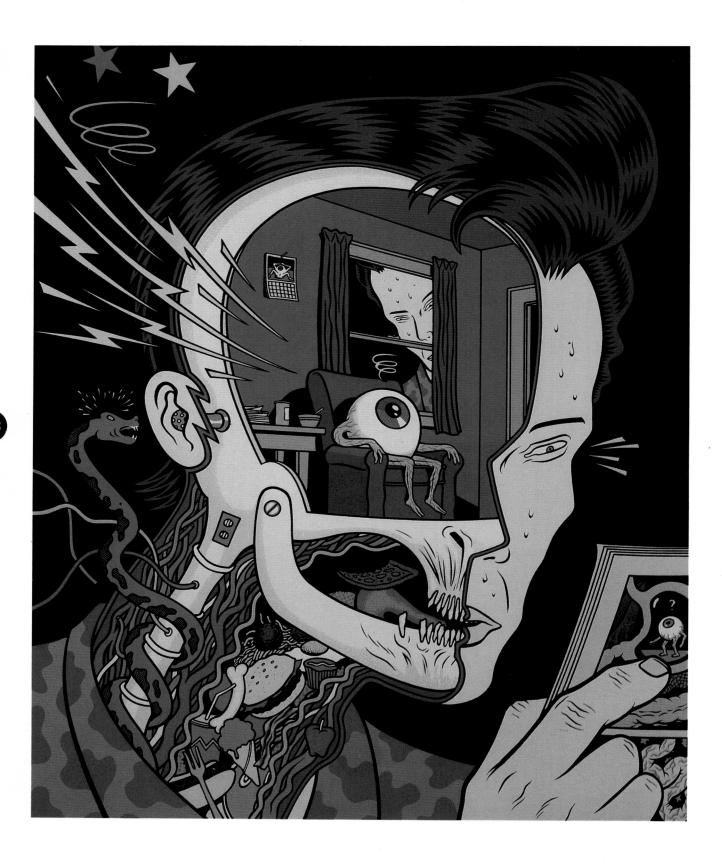

138

139

THERE ARE THREE WATERING HOLES IN THIS PLACE ON THE COAST AND NOTHING ELSE TO DO IN THE CRUSHING HEAT BUT COMPARE THE INTRINSIC QUALITIES OF THE ESTABLISHMENTS, PINK, WHITE AND BLUE RESPECTIVELY.

140

THE SHOWERS ARE IN AN ADJACENT STRUCTURE. WHEN YOU GO THERE, IT'S WISE TO AVOID MEETING THE DUTCH NUDIST NAMED HANSI, SHOWN IN THE NEXT PANEL.

jacques Loustal

IT IS HANSI'S CUSTOM TO GO SWIMMING TWICE A DAY, NO MATTER HOW COLD THE WATER IS. AFTER HIS SWIM HE LAUGHS VERY LOUDLY, THUMPING HIS GRANITE TORSO.

THERE ARE CHAIRS SET OUT ON THE TERRACE, AND THE TOURIST THOUGHT IT MIGHT BE A SUITABLE SPOT FOR MEDITATION. BUT HIS MIND CLOUDED OVER, AS THE HOURS AND THE BEERS WENT BY, WITHOUT PRODUCING A SINGLE COHERENT REFLECTION.

THE WHITE BAR LOOKS OUT OVER THE OCEAN; FROM THERE THE TRAVELER
OBSERVED AT LENGTH THE RHYTHM AND VOLUME OF THE WAVES.
"THE SEVENTH IS ALWAYS THE LARGEST," HE NOTED TO HIMSELF.

ALL ALCOHOL CONSUMPTION IS DONE IN HIDING, IN A DARK ROOM WHERE THE
DRINKERS LINE UP EMPTY BOTTLES OF "STORK" ON THE TABLE, SOMETIMES
TEN AT A TIME.
SMOKY ATMOSPHERE, PERSISTENT GAZES.

THE "MIRAMAR" IS RUN BY A SWARTHY, FULL-BOSOMED WIDOW, SHOWN
IN THE NEXT PANEL.
THE WALLS ARE HUNG WITH PAINTINGS IN THE NAÏF STYLE, CREATED BY
HER DECEASED HUSBAND.

THIS WOMAN WITH HER AMPLE FLESH AND EXCESSIVELY SENSUAL PHYSIQUE
PROVED TO BE VERY UNDERSTANDING TOWARD THE TRAVELER ONE EVENING
WHEN HE WAS DEPRESSED.

Living coLor

129 **VANITY**
by Lorenzo Mattotti

Italy's most sumptuous New Comics artist find his own unique style somewhere between the world of fashion illustration, and the world of narrative comics.

133 **GLOOM**
by Richard Sala

Post modern mystery writing in given a vital Spanish twist in the art world of Berkeley's Richard Sala.

134 **JIMMY RODGERS**
by Lynda Barry

The folk world of rural America is invoked in this loving, beautifully laced, tribute to the life and times of the "Singing Brakeman."

136 **HOT ROD TALES**
by Robert Williams

The violent world of pre-Low Rider Los Angeles is brought back to life in the modern folk art paintings by this former contributor to the legendary *Zap* magazine.

138 **TWO COVERS**
by Charles Burns

Two rare magazine covers from one of the reigning geniuses of American comics *noir*, Philadelphia's elegantly twisted Charles Burns.

140 **OCEAN VIEW**
by Jacques Loustal

In its first English-language publication, a sense of grit you can almost taste, and a rare sensuousness, informs this modern French tale of a lonely Dutch tourist who finds new love in a largely deserted North African town.

144 **BABYLAND BABYLON**
by David Sandlin

Child of James Brown, and Elvis; beyond all drive-in movies, travelling carnivals, and amusement parks, the spirit king of rural America rises in evangelical splendor to join the original honky tonk choir in the heavens.

the best new comics adventure tales begin where the great e.c. war and horror comics left off in the 1950s. an even darker sense of realism, and a far more sophisticated sense of political reality, now characterize the best of these stories. in the works of willem, sacco, spain & o'neill, we see the beginnings of a new graphic journalism. in the crime fictions of loustal, munoz & sampayo, and tardi we find a fascinating **roman noir** school of comic strip writing now beginning to unfold.

tales of
politics & crime

148 LONDON'S CHANGED
by Gary and Warren Pleece
Forecasting the fate of too many returning Vietnam veterans in the U.S.A, the returning World War One veteran in this story finds that he is invisible in post-war Great Britain.

154 WHEN GOOD BOMBS HAPPEN TO BAD PEOPLE
by Joe Sacco
In a story published before the outbreak of the recent Gulf War, Joe Sacco provides a short history of the major bombing campaigns since World War Two.

162 JERUSALEM
by Bernhard (Willem) Holstrop
The great Liberation cartoonist Willem creates a documentary introduction to the terror and the politics of the Mid-East.

168 PSYCHOLOGICAL OPERATIONS IN GUERRILLA WAR
by Carel Moseiwitch
Canada's Carel Moseiwitch examines the late William Casey's small literary gift to the people of Nicaragua.

170 THE BLACK FREIGHTER
by Cliff Harper
England's Cliff Harper translates Brecht into a comic strip, and finds new meaning in a powerful old song.

174 BELFAST
by Dan O'Neill
The legendary creator of "Odd Bodkins" paints a particularly haunting portrait inside the war zone in beleagured Northern Ireland.

175 DURRUTI
by Spain (Rodriquez)
The life and times of a neglected Spanish Civil War hero as profiled by this legendary San Francisco underground cartoonist.

180 THE "COCKEYED" COOK STORY
by Mark Zingarelli
The true life adventures of Wiliam Edward Cook are reconstructed by this brilliant Pacific Northwest Coast artist.

187 DENNIS THE SULLEN MENACE
by Dennis Eichhorn & Michael Dougan
Two of Seattle's finest New Comics artists combine to provide a haunting penitentiary tale of life on murderer's row.

193 34 PENN STATION
by Munoz & Sampayo
Argentina's most talented crime writing team visit the subways of New York City in this previously untranslated homage to Thomas Wolfe.

195 THE LAW
by Marti (Riera)
In its first English language appearance, live in a surreal, future police state is depicted by Spain's finest contemporary crime strip writer.

198 STALINGRAD
by Colin Upton
Delirium turns into holy Gnostic script in this brilliant story by one of Canada's most talented younger comics writers.

202 TICKET, S.V.P!
by Marc Caro
The futuristic tone is carried one step further in the first English translation of this contemporary classic by France's young master of the post-modern terrorist tale.

208 THE MURDERER OF HUNG
by Dominque Grange and Jacques Tardi
The lessons of Viet Nam are played out on the streets of Manhatten in this powerful story by journalist Domique Grange, and the master of the French roman noir graphic style, Jacques Tardi.

THE TRAIN GOT US BACK INTO LONDON RATHER LATER THAN EXPECTED...

STILL, BETTER LATE THAN NEVER....

ISN'T THAT WHAT I ALWAYS SAID?

I *THINK* IT'S GOOD TO BE BACK....

THE NOISE THESE LONDON STREETS MAKE HOWEVER IS SOME— HOW ALL TOO FAMILIAR.

IT'S A *DIFFERENT KIND OF BATTLE* OVER HERE THOUGH.

IT'D BE EASY TO SAY THINGS AIN'T WHAT THEY USED TO BE ...SO I'LL SAY IT...

"things ain't what they used to be!"

LONDON'S CHANGED

I DON'T EVER REMEMBER IT BEING BEAUTIFUL HERE...

BUT THERE'S SOMETHING EVEN LESS BEAUTIFUL ABOUT IT NOW.

WENT TO SEE A NEW PLAY AT THE DOMINION.

CORNY, FAKE + FRENCH

"A RIP ROARER"
— DAILY MIRROR

"THE KRAUTS WILL BE SOUR, BUT WE BEEFY BRITS WILL LOVE IT!!"
— THE SUN

"FUCKING CRAP"
— THE INDEPENDENT

'FUNNILY ENOUGH (OR, SHOULD I SAY, UNFUNNILY ENOUGH) IT WAS SUPPOSED TO BE A SATIRE ABOUT THE RESISTANCE'S INVOLVEMENT DURING THE WAR...

HOW MANY WARS HAVE THERE BEEN?

'TIZ ALL RIGHT. 'E IZ ONLY A ZOUR KRAUT WITH A TINY ZAUZAGE BETWEEN IZ LEGZ!

'TIZ OKAY! A NIBBLE ON A ZAUZAGE IZ ALL I VANT! I'M NOT STARVING!

HA HA HA!

THEY NEEDED SHOOTING FOR SOME OF THE 'JOKES'!

HOW CAN YOU LAUGH AT THAT, YOU BASTARDS!

UNFORTUNATELY, I WAS ALWAYS A LOUSY SHOT, EH, FELLAS?

I USUALLY FIND THAT IT PUTS SUCH A DAMPENER ON DINNER PARTIES.

REALLY? NOT FOR ME. AS LONG AS THE FOOD'S ITALIAN, I'M WEARING MY BEST FROM 'NEXT', THE BULGARIAN RED IS FLOWING AND DAVID'S GOT HIS COLOMBIAN MARIJUANA.... I FIND PERIODS INCONSEQUENTIAL.

HALT!

151

GET OUT THE WAY!

GET OUT THE WAY!

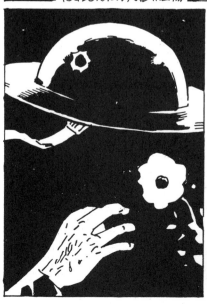

When GOOD BOMBS happen to BAD PEOPLE

by Joe Sacco 1990

J SACCO 9-90

BRITISH BOMBING OF GERMANY, 1940-45

"BOMBS ARE NOT TO BE DROPPED INDISCRIMINATELY."
—BOMBER COMMAND, JUNE '40

"THE ATTACK MUST BE MADE WITH REASONABLE CARE TO AVOID UNDUE LOSS OF CIVIL LIFE IN THE VICINITY OF THE TARGET."
—REVISED INSTRUCTION TO AIR MINISTRY, JUNE '40

"WE HAVE SEEN WHAT INCONVENIENCE THE ATTACK ON THE BRITISH POPULATION HAS CAUSED US, AND THERE IS NO REASON WHY THE ENEMY SHOULD BE FREE FROM ALL SUCH EMBARRASSMENTS."
—PRIME MINISTER CHURCHILL TO AIR MINISTRY, NOV. '40

"YOU ARE ACCORDINGLY AUTHORIZED TO EMPLOY YOUR FORCES WITHOUT RESTRICTION. OPERATIONS... SHOULD NOW BE FOCUSED ON THE MORALE OF THE ENEMY CIVIL POPULATION AND IN PARTICULAR OF THE INDUSTRIAL WORKER."
—AIR MINISTRY, FEB. '42

"REF THE NEW BOMBING DIRECTIVE: I SUPPOSE IT IS CLEAR THAT THE AIMING-POINTS ARE TO BE THE BUILT-UP AREAS, NOT, FOR INSTANCE, THE DOCK-YARDS AND AIRCRAFT FACTORIES.... THIS MUST BE MADE QUITE CLEAR IF IT IS NOT ALREADY UNDERSTOOD."
—AIR CHIEF-MARSHAL PORTAL, FEB. '42

"... ONE TON OF BOMBS DROPPED ON A BUILT-UP AREA DEMOLISHES 20-40 DWELLINGS AND TURNS 100-200 PEOPLE OUT OF HOUSE AND HOME.... WE CAN COUNT ON NEARLY 14 OPERATIONAL SORTIES PER BOMBER PRODUCED. THE AVERAGE LIFT OF THE BOMBERS ... WILL BE ABOUT THREE TONS. IT FOLLOWS THAT EACH OF THESE BOMBERS WILL IN ITS LIFETIME DROP ABOUT FORTY TONS OF BOMBS. IF THESE ARE DROPPED ON BUILT-UP AREAS THEY WILL MAKE 4,000-8,000 PEOPLE HOMELESS...."
—LORD CHERWELL, SCIENTIFIC ADVISER TO CHURCHILL, MAR. '42

"SLOWLY HIS FOREFINGER MOVED ACROSS THE MAP, OVER THE CONTINENT OF EUROPE UNTIL IT CAME TO REST ON A TOWN IN GERMANY .... HE TURNED TO SAUNDBY, HIS FACE STILL EXPRESSIONLESS. "'THE THOUSAND-PLAN — TONIGHT.' "HIS FINGER PRESSED ON COLOGNE AS HE SPOKE."
—ON BOMBER COMMAND C-IN-C ARTHUR HARRIS, MAY 30, '42

"...AN HOUR AND A HALF AS NO CITY ON EARTH HAD EVER BEFORE UNDERGONE. EVERY SIX SECONDS ANOTHER BRITISH BOMBER ROARED OVER THE DOOMED RHINELAND CENTER."
—NEWSWEEK, JUNE '42

"WE ARE GOING TO SCOURGE THE THIRD REICH FROM END TO END. WE ARE BOMBING GERMANY CITY BY CITY AND EVER MORE TERRIBLY IN ORDER TO MAKE IT IMPOSSIBLE FOR HER TO GO ON WITH THE WAR. THAT IS OUR OBJECTIVE; WE WILL PURSUE IT RELENT-LESSLY."
—HARRIS

"USE OF THESE NEW BOMBS UNDERLINED THE LARGELY UNPUBLICIZED BUT IMMENSELY IMPORTANT ROLE THAT INCEN-DIARIES ARE PLAYING IN RAF* RAIDS ON THE REICH....IT MAY BE THAT GERMANY'S FATE IS TO BE BURNED DOWN RATHER THAN BLOWN UP."
—NEWSWEEK, JULY '43

"OPERATION GOMORRAH."
— CODE NAME FOR RAIDS ON HAMBURG, JULY 24-AUG.2, '43

"NEUTRAL EUROPEAN NEWS-PAPERS PRINTED STORIES OF THE HORROR AND DESOLATION OF THE CHARNEL STENCH THAT WAS HAMBURG. THESE STORIES OF WIDESPREAD DESTRUCTION WERE PROBABLY INSPIRED BY BERLIN IN THE HOPE OF MIS-LEADING THE ALLIES INTO THINKING THAT THEY HAD DESTROYED MORE THAN THEY REALLY HAD AND THAT HAMBURG NEEDED NO FURTHER ATTENTION FROM THE AIR."
—LIFE, AUG. '43

KILLED IN HAMBURG RAIDS: 31-50,000

"... 2,400,000,000 [ENEMY] MAN-HOURS HAVE BEEN LOST FOR THE EXPENDITURE OF 116,500 TONS OF BOMBS CLAIMED DROPPED, AND THIS AMOUNTS TO AN AVERAGE RETURN FOR EVERY TON OF BOMBS DROPPED OF 20,500 LOST MAN-HOURS, OR RATHER MORE THAN ONE QUARTER OF THE TIME SPENT IN BUILDING A LANCASTER [BOMBER]....THIS BEING SO, A LANCASTER HAS ONLY TO GO TO A GERMAN CITY ONCE TO WIPE OFF ITS OWN CAPITAL COST, AND THE RESULT OF ALL SUBSEQUENT SORTIES WILL BE CLEAR PROFIT."
—AIR STAFF INTELLIGENCE REPORT, FEB.'44

"NOT INCLUDING THE SUBURBS, A DESTRUCTION OF LESS THAN 40 PER CENT OF BUILT-UP AREA IS ENOUGH TO MAKE A CITY UNPRODUCTIVE."
—HARRIS

"THESE BOMBINGS ARE NOT A SAVAGE RETALIATION....IT IS A CONSIDERED POLICY WITH ONE AIM IN VIEW: TO FORCE THE SURRENDER OF THE GERMAN GOVERNMENT AT THE EARLIEST POSSIBLE MOMENT AND HENCE WITH THE LEAST POSSIBLE TOTAL LOSS OF LIFE....TOTAL WAR MEANS JUST THAT. UNIFORMS NO LONGER MASK COMBATANTS. THERE ARE NO NON-COMBATANTS."
— SENIOR SCHOLASTIC, APRIL '44

"...IN THE PAST EIGHTEEN MONTHS, BOMBER COMMAND HAS VIRTUALLY DESTROYED FORTY-FIVE OUT OF THE LEADING SIXTY GERMAN CITIES. IN SPITE OF INVASION DIVERSIONS WE HAVE SO FAR MANAGED TO KEEP UP AND EVEN EXCEED OUR AVERAGE OF TWO AND A HALF CITIES DEVASTATED A MONTH... THERE ARE NOT MANY INDUS- TRIAL CENTERS OF POPULATION NOW LEFT INTACT."
—HARRIS, NOV. '44

"THE TIME MIGHT WELL COME IN THE NOT TOO DISTANT FUTURE WHEN AN ALL-OUT ATTACK BY EVERY MEANS AT OUR DISPOSAL ON GERMAN CIVILIAN MORALE MIGHT BE DECISIVE."
— BRITISH CHIEF OF STAFF TO CHURCHILL, JULY '44

"IF WE ASSUME THAT THE DAYTIME POPULATION OF THE AREA ATTACKED IS 300,000, WE MAY EXPECT 220,000 CASUALTIES. 50 PERCENT OF THESE OR 110,000 MAY EXPECT TO BE KILLED. IT IS SUGGESTED THAT SUCH AN ATTACK RESULTING IN SO MANY DEATHS, THE GREAT PROPORTION OF WHICH WILL BE KEY PERSONNEL, CANNOT HELP BUT HAVE A SHATTERING EFFECT ON POLITICAL AND CIVILIAN MORALE ALL OVER GERMANY...."
—DIRECTORATE OF BOMBER OPERATIONS, SUMMER '41.

"IN BOMBER COMMAND WE HAVE ALWAYS WORKED ON THE ASSUMPTION THAT BOMBING ANYTHING IN GERMANY IS BETTER THAN BOMBING NOTHING."
—HARRIS, FALL '44

"I DID NOT ASK YOU LAST NIGHT ABOUT PLANS FOR HARRYING THE GERMAN RETREAT FROM BRESLAU. ON THE CON- TRARY, I ASKED WHETHER BERLIN, AND NO DOUBT OTHER LARGE CITIES IN EAST GERMANY, SHOULD NOT NOW BE CONSIDERED ESPECIALLY ATTRACTIVE TARGETS. I AM GLAD THIS IS 'UNDER EXAM- INATION.' PRAY REPORT TO ME TOMORROW WHAT IS GOING TO BE DONE."
—CHURCHILL TO SEC. OF STATE IN THE AIR, JAN. '45

"...2250 UNITED STATES HEAVY BOMBERS AND FIGHTERS RANGED OVER GERMANY IN WIDESPREAD RAIDS, DELIVERING THEIR MAIN ATTACK ON THIS REFUGEE-PACKED CAPITAL OF SAXONY.
"THE AMERICAN AIR STRIKES CAME IN THE WAKE OF BLOWS BY 1400 RAF BOMBERS DURING THE NIGHT....[DRESDEN] WAS STILL BURNING WHEN AMERICAN PLANES ARRIVED LATER IN THE DAY."
—ASSOCIATED PRESS, FEB. 15, '45

KILLED IN DRESDEN RAIDS: 25–135,000

"THE ALLIED AIR BOSSES HAVE MADE THE LONG-AWAITED DECISION TO ADOPT DELIBERATE TERROR BOMBING OF THE GERMAN POPULATION CENTERS AS A RUTHLESS EXPEDIENT TO HASTEN HITLER'S DOOM."
—ASSOCIATED PRESS, FEB 18, '45

U.S. BOMBING OF JAPAN, 1944-45

"...ANY GENERAL BOMBING OF AN EXTENSIVE AREA WHEREIN THERE RESIDES A LARGE POPULATION ENGAGED IN PEACEFUL PURSUITS IS UNWARRANTED AND CONTRARY TO PRINCIPLES OF LAW AND OF HUMANITY."
—U.S. DEPT. OF STATE, SEPT. '37

"[I] RECALL WITH PRIDE THAT THE UNITED STATES CONSISTENTLY HAS TAKEN THE LEAD IN URGING THAT THIS INHUMAN PRACTICE BE PROHIBITED."
—PRESIDENT ROOSEVELT, '40

"[THE USE] OF INCENDIARIES AGAINST CITIES WAS CONTRARY TO OUR NATIONAL POLICY OF ATTACKING ONLY MILITARY OBJECTIVES."
—GENERAL 'HAP' ARNOLD, '40

"[JAPANESE] TOWNS ARE BUILT LARGELY OF WOOD AND PAPER TO RESIST THE DEVESTATIONS OF EARTHQUAKES AND FORM THE GREATEST AERIAL TARGETS THE WORLD HAS EVER SEEN.... INCENDIARY PROJECTILES WOULD BURN THE CITIES TO THE GROUND IN SHORT ORDER."
—GENERAL 'BILLY' MITCHELL, 31

"THE JAPANESE LITERALLY LIVE IN A HOUSE OF TINDER.... INCENDIARY BOMBS ARE NIPPON'S NIGHTMARE. FEAR OF FIRE IS BRED IN THE PEOPLE....IN A GREAT CONGESTED CITY LIKE TOKYO, WITH ITS 7,000,000 PEOPLE ...GREAT SECTIONS... ARE LIKE KINDLING WOOD."
—NY TIMES MAG., APRIL '42

"THE POSSIBILITIES INHERENT IN INCENDIARY BOMBING HAVE GREATLY BRIGHTENED IN RECENT MONTHS....BETTER AND BETTER INCENDIARIES ARE BECOMING AVAILABLE."
—V.P. OF STANDARD OIL DEVELOPMENT, SEPT. '42

"ESTIMATES OF ECONOMIC DAMAGE EXPECTED INDICATE THAT INCENDIARY ATTACK OF JAPANESE CITIES MAY BE AT LEAST FIVE TIMES AS EFFECTIVE, TON FOR TON, AS PRECISION BOMBING....HOWEVER, THE DRY ECONOMIC STATISTICS, IMPRESSIVE AS THEY MAY BE, STILL DO NOT TAKE ACCOUNT OF THE FURTHER AND UNPREDICTABLE EFFECT ON THE JAPANESE WAR EFFORT OF A NATIONAL CATASTROPHE OF SUCH MAGNITUDE—ENTIRELY UNPRECEDENTED IN HISTORY."
—OFFICE OF SCIENTIFIC RESEARCH AND DEVELOPMENT RECOMMENDATION, FALL '44

"THE SUBCOMMITTEE CONSIDERED AN OPTIMUM RESULT OF COMPLETE CHAOS IN SIX [JAPANESE] CITIES KILLING 584,000 PEOPLE."
—COLONEL JOHN F. TURNER, INCENDIARY SUBCOMMITTEE, COMMITTEE OF OPERATIONS ANALYSTS.

J. SACCO 9 90

"CIVILIANS! EVACUATE AT ONCE! "THESE LEAFLETS ARE BEING DROPPED TO NOTIFY YOU THAT YOUR CITY HAS BEEN LISTED FOR DESTRUCTION BY OUR POWERFUL AIR FORCE. THE BOMBING WILL OCCUR WITHIN 72 HOURS. THIS ADVANCE NOTICE WILL GIVE YOUR MILITARY AUTHORITIES AMPLE TIME TO TAKE NECESSARY DEFENSIVE MEASURES TO PROTECT YOU FROM INEVITABLE ATTACK. WATCH AND SEE HOW POWERLESS THEY ARE TO PROTECT YOU...."
—FROM LEAFLET DROPPED BY B-29S SUMMER, '45

"IF THIS RAID WORKS THE WAY I THINK IT WILL, WE CAN SHORTEN THE WAR."
-GEN. CURTIS LEMAY, MAR. '45

"A BLANKET OF FIRE WAS THROWN OVER AN AREA OF FIFTEEN SQUARE MILES IN THE HEART OF TOKYO EARLY TODAY BY A FLEET OF 300 B-29'S IN THE LARGEST AND MOST INTENSIFIED RAID ON THAT CITY TO DATE."
—NY TIMES, MAR. 10, '45

"... I CAN SAY WITH CON-SERVATISM THAT THIS LOOKS GOOD FROM OUR POINT OF VIEW AND GRIM FROM THE POINT OF VIEW OF THE ENEMY. THERE IS A CON-FLAGRATION IN TOKYO TONIGHT."
-GEN. LEMAY, MAR. 10, '45

"BY NOON LEMAY WAS SURE HE HAD WHAT HE LIKES TO CALL A 'DILLER'."
-FORTUNE, OCT. '45

"A DREAM CAME TRUE LAST WEEK FOR U.S. ARMY AVIATORS; THEY GOT THEIR CHANCE TO LOOSE AVALANCHES OF FIRE BOMBS ON TOKYO AND NOGOYA, AND THEY PROVED THAT, PROPERLY KINDLED, JAPANESE CITIES WILL BURN LIKE AUTUMN LEAVES."
-TIME, MAR. '45

RESULT OF MARCH 10, 1945, TOKYO RAID:
  80-130,000 KILLED
  41,000 INJURED
  1,000,000 HOMELESS

"SMALL, INEFFECTIVE RAIDS, SPACED ABOUT TWO WEEKS APART AT FIRST, HAD GROWN TO 400-PLANE RAIDS AT TWO-DAY INTERVALS.... NEW U.S. FIRE BOMBS HAVE PROVED TO BE A WHITE-HOT SUCCESS."
-TIME, MAY '45

"AT THE END OF JULY ONLY FOUR BOMBERS HAD BEEN LOST IN THE LAST THREE THOUSAND SORTIES. THIS IS AIR WAR ACCORDING TO THE TEXTBOOKS—THE PROGRESSIVE ANNIHILATION OF ONE NATION WITHOUT MUCH AIR POWER BY ANOTHER WITH PRACTICALLY UNLIMITED STRENGTH."
-FORTUNE, SEPT. '45

"WE DIDN'T HEAR ANY COM-PLAINTS FROM THE AMERICAN PEOPLE ABOUT MASS BOMBING OF JAPAN; AS A MATTER OF FACT, I THINK THEY FELT THE MORE WE DID THE BETTER."
-GENERAL CARL SPAATZ

"THERE ARE NO INNOCENT CIVILIANS. IT IS THEIR GOVERN-MENT AND YOU ARE FIGHTING A PEOPLE, YOU ARE NOT TRY-ING TO FIGHT AN ARMED FORCE ANYMORE. SO IT DOESN'T BOTHER ME SO MUCH TO BE KILLING INNOCENT BYSTANDERS."
-GENERAL LEMAY

"THE ENTIRE POPULATION OF JAPAN IS A PROPER MILITARY TARGET....THERE ARE NO CIVILIANS IN JAPAN."
-5TH AIR FORCE WEEKLY INTELLIGENCE REVIEW, JULY'45

joe sacco

U.S. BOMBING OF LIBYA, APRIL 14, 1986

"TOM, TRIPOLI IS UNDER ATTACK."
—STEVE DELANEY TO TOM BROKAW, ABC NEWS, 7:02 EST

"PUT YOUR MICROPHONE OUT THAT WINDOW AND LET US HEAR IT."
—DAN RATHER TO JEFFREY FAGER, CBS NEWS

"THE RAID BEGAN AROUND 7 P.M. MONDAY WASHINGTON TIME...AND WAS OVER IN TIME FOR A WHITE HOUSE ANNOUNCEMENT TO CATCH EVENING T.V. NEWS SHOWS."
—TIME

"MY FELLOW AMERICANS, AT 7 O'CLOCK THIS EVENING EASTERN TIME, AIR AND NAVAL FORCES OF THE UNITED STATES LAUNCHED STRIKES AGAINST THE HEAD-QUARTERS, TERRORIST FACIL-ITIES AND MILITARY ASSETS THAT SUPPORT MUAMMAR QADDAFI'S SUBVERSIVE ACTIVITIES....
"THE EVIDENCE IS NOW CONCLUSIVE THAT THE TERRORIST BOMBING OF THE LA BELLE DISCOTHEQUE WAS PLANNED AND EXECUTED UNDER DIRECT ORDERS OF THE LIBYAN REGIME...."
—PRESIDENT RONALD REAGAN

"LIBYA BEARS DIRECT RES-PONSIBILITY FOR THE [DISCO] BOMBING IN WEST BERLIN ON APRIL 5 THAT RESULTED IN THE DEATH OF ARMY SGT. KENNETH FORD AND INJURY TO A NUMBER OF AMERICAN SERVICEMEN AND OTHERS...."
—WHITEHOUSE SPOKES-PERSON LARRY SPEAKES

"VERY, VERY CLEAR EVIDENCE THAT THERE IS LIBYAN INVOLVEMENT."
—U.S. AMBASSADOR TO W. GERMANY RICHARD BURT

"THE AMERICAN REPRESENT-ATIVE WAS UNABLE TO CITE ANY FACTUAL EVIDENCE IN SUPPORT OF HIS ALLEGATIONS."
—SOVIET FOREIGN MINISTRY SPOKESPERSON V. LOMEIKO

"OUR EVIDENCE IS DIRECT, IT IS PRECISE, IT IS IRREFUTABLE...."
—PRESIDENT REAGAN

"I HAVE NO MORE EVIDENCE THAT LIBYA WAS CONNECTED TO THE [DISCO] BOMBING THAN I HAD WHEN YOU FIRST CALLED ME TWO DAYS AFTER THE ACT. WHICH IS NONE."
—MANFRED GANSCHOW, HEAD OF 100-MAN TEAM INVESTIG-ATING THE DISCO BOMBING

"WE ARE BEYOND THE POINT WHERE WE HAVE TO PRODUCE COURTROOM MATERIALS ON QADDAFI."
—UNNAMED "SENIOR OFFICIAL"

Q: "WAS THERE AN EFFORT, SIR, TO GET QADDAFI PERSONALLY?"
SEC. OF DEFENSE CASPAR WEINBERGER: "NO THERE WAS NOT."

159

"WE ALL KNOW WHAT YOU DO WITH A MAD DOG."
 -UNNAMED "SENIOR U.S. OFFICIAL"

160

"... THERE APPEARED TO BE EIGHT BOMB CRATERS ALONG A 300-YARD ROW EXTENDING FROM IMMEDIATELY IN FRONT OF THE COLONEL'S HOUSE TO AN ADMINISTRATIVE BUILDING UNDER WHICH HE WORKS IN A FORTIFIED BUNKER. THE ROW PASSED WITHIN 50 YARDS OF A CAMOUFLAGED BEDOUIN TENT IN WHICH THE COLONEL ALSO WORKS."
 -NY TIMES

"WE ARE NOT TRYING TO GO AFTER QADDAFI AS SUCH, ALTHOUGH WE THINK HE IS A RULER THAT IS BETTER OUT OF HIS COUNTRY."
 -SEC. OF STATE GEORGE SHULTZ

"NO FEWER THAN FIVE F-111S WERE ASSIGNED TO HIT QADDAFI'S COMPOUND."
 -TIME

"THE UNITED STATES IS NEITHER TRYING TO KILL QADDAFI NOR REPLACE HIS REGIME WITH A GOVERNMENT MORE FAVORABLE TO THE UNITED STATES."
 -STATE DEPT. SPOKESPERSON BERNARD KALB

"AMONG THOSE REPORTED DEAD WAS COLONEL QADDAFI'S 15-MONTH-OLD ADOPTED DAUGHTER.... HIS DAUGHTER, HANA, DIED TWO AND A HALF HOURS AFTER SUFFERING A CONCUSSION AND INTERNAL INJURIES FROM AN EXPLOSION NEXT TO THE COLONEL'S HOME.... THE TWO INJURED SONS OF COLONEL QADDAFI'S SEVEN SURVIVING CHILDREN WERE LISTED IN SERIOUS CONDITION.... QADDAFI'S WIFE 'WAS IN A BAD STATE OF SHOCK.'"
 -NY TIMES

"ACCORDING TO ONE OF HIS INTIMATES, THE PRESIDENT WAS UPSET WHEN U.S. INTELLIGENCE INDICATED THAT THE RAID ON TRIPOLI HAD KILLED ONE OF QADDAFI'S CHILDREN. 'THE ONE THING THAT GETS TO HIM IS CARNAGE,' THE SOURCE SAYS."
 -NEWSWEEK

"WE WEREN'T OUT TO KILL ANYBODY."
 -PRESIDENT REAGAN

"WE WERE STRIKING AT HIM PERSONALLY, NOT THAT HE WAS THE TARGET.....WE KNEW THAT THAT WAS HIS RESIDENCE AND THAT HE PERHAPS MIGHT BE THERE AND MEMBERS OF HIS FAMILY."
 -UNNAMED "SENIOR WHITE HOUSE AIDE"

"[SHULTZ] NOTED THAT AMERICAN REGULATIONS BAR ASSASSINATIONS OF FOREIGN LEADERS."
 -NY TIMES

"A BILL AUTHORIZING THE PRESIDENT TO RESPOND TO FOREIGN TERRORISM WITHOUT CONSULTING CONGRESS IN ADVANCE WAS INTRODUCED BY REPUBLICANS... TODAY.... THE BILL WOULD APPARENTLY PERMIT THE

PRESIDENT TO ORDER THE ASSASSINATION OF A FOREIGN LEADER UNDER SOME CIRCUMSTANCES.... SENATOR DENTON SAID THAT IF COL. MUAMMAR EL-QADDAFI 'BECAME DECEASED AS A RESULT OF OUR COUNTERSTRIKE, THAT WOULD HAVE BEEN WITHIN THE INTENT OF THE BILL.'"
          -NY TIMES

"A TONE OF RELIEF AND REVENGE RAN THROUGH MANY COMMENTS, AS CONGRESSMEN COMPETED WITH ONE ANOTHER TO DENOUNCE LIBYA AND ITS LEADER...."
          -NY TIMES

"A GREEK DOCTOR, HIS FACE AND WRIST PATCHED UP WITH BAND-AIDS, LIMPED DOWN THE STREET, SAYING HIS WIFE WAS STILL IN THE HOSPITAL AND MUMBLING PROFANITIES ABOUT THE UNITED STATES."
          -NY TIMES

"WE'RE JUST NOT GOING TO LET AMERICANS BE TERRORIZED AROUND THE WORLD."
-HOUSE SPEAKER 'TIP' O'NEILL

"TAHER MOHAMMED GUBBIA, HIS VOICE SHAKING IN RAGE, CALLED IT TERRORISM. HE SAID THE AMERICAN FIGHTER BOMBERS DESTROYED HIS HOME EARLY THIS MORNING. HIS WIFE'S ARM WAS BROKEN IN THE ATTACK.... AT LEAST 15 OF MR. GUBBIA'S NEIGHBORS WERE KILLED...."
          -NY TIMES

"... A BRAVE, BALANCED AND BOLD DECISION TO RETALIATE IN THE DEFENSE OF FREEDOM AGAINST THE ONSLAUGHT OF A HOSTILE TOTALITARIAN REGIME THAT IS A PARIAH IN THE WORLD COMMUNITY."
   -SENATOR DAN QUAYLE

"AT THE DOOR LAY THE BODY OF A LITTLE GIRL.... BESIDE HER WAS AN INFANT IN A PINK PLAYSUIT. BETWEEN THEM LAY TWO SMALL HANDS, SEVERED JUST BELOW THE WRIST."
          -NEWSWEEK

"...EVEN THE MOST SCRUPULOUS CITIZEN CAN ONLY APPROVE AND APPLAUD THE AMERICAN ATTACKS ON LIBYA.... IF THERE WERE SUCH A THING AS DUE PROCESS IN THE COURT OF WORLD OPINION, THE UNITED STATES HAS OBSERVED IT...."
     -NY TIMES EDITORIAL

"AS FAR AS WHAT WE CALL THE BOMBING OPTION IS CONCERNED, THAT CANNOT BE USED AGAIN UNLESS IT IS MASSIVE.... WITH QADDAFI I THINK WE DID THE RIGHT THING AT THAT TIME, BUT FROM NOW ON WE'VE GOT TO THINK IN BIGGER TERMS."
   -FORMER PRESIDENT NIXON

■ israel

■ arabes ■ palestine ■ liban ■

israel ■

bernhard (willem) holstrop

THE PALESTINE POLICE FORCE.

WANTED!

REWARDS WILL BE PAID BY THE PALESTINE GOVERNMENT TO ANY PERSON PROVIDING INFORMATION WHICH LEADS TO THE ARREST OF ANY OF THE PERSONS WHOSE NAMES AND PHOTOGRAPHS ARE SHOWN HEREUNDER.

ITZHAK YEZERNITSKY

Age : 32 years
Height : 165 cm
Build : Heavy
Complexion : Sallow
Hair : Brown
Eyes : Brown

THE PALESTINE
POST
CARL MARX

STATE OF ISRAEL IS BORN

Most Crowded Hours in Palestine's History | JEWS TAKE OVER SECURITY ZONES | Egyptian Air Force Spitfires Bomb Tel Aviv; One Shot Down | U.S. RECOGNIZES JEWISH STATE | Proclamation by Head Of Government

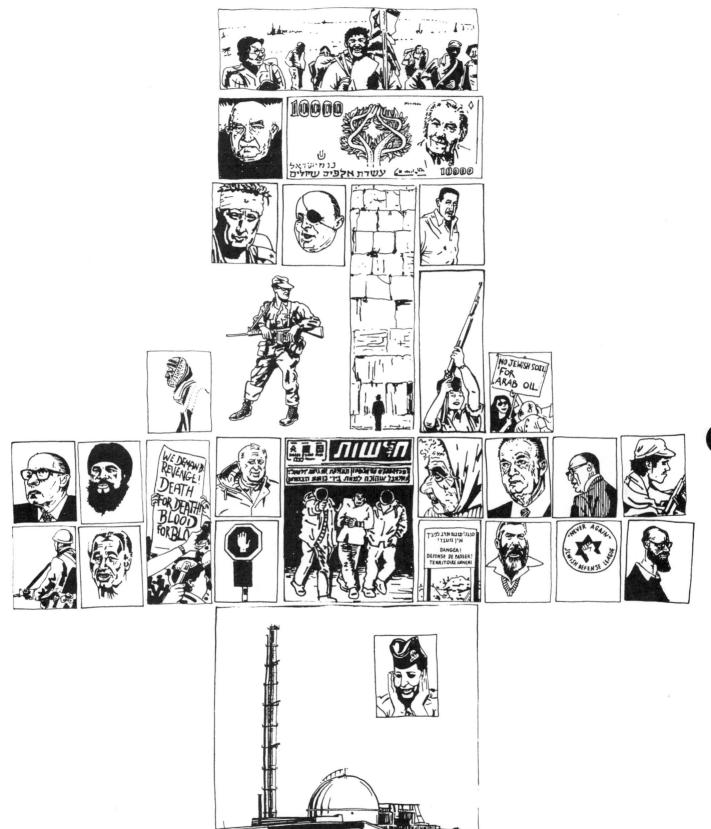

carel moseiwitch

THE BLACK FREIGHTER
WORDS-BERT BRECHT ART-CLIFF HARPER

You gentlemen can gawk, while i'm scrubbing the floors
and scrubbing the floors, why are you gawking?

And maybe once you tipped me, and it made you feel swell
In this ratty water pub in this ratty hotel

And you'll never know to whom you're talking
You'll never guess to whom you're talking

Suddenly one night there's a scream in the night
And you yell what the hell is that din?

And you see me kinda grinning while i'm scrubbing
And you say what she got to grin?

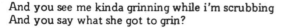

*AND THE SHIP, THE BLACK FREIGHTER
WITH THE SKULL AND THE CROSSPATCH*

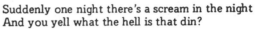

SAILS INTO THE BAY

cliff Harper

Then you gentlemen can say, hey girl scrub the floor
Make the beds, clean down the stair, earn your keep here

And you pass out of the house
and you look out at the ships
And i'm counting the heads and i'm making them stick

Cos tonight none of you will sleep here
Tonight none of you will sleep here

Then on that night there's a bang in the night
And you yell what the hell is that row?

And you'll see me kinda staring out the window
And you'll say whats she got to stare at now?

*AND THE SHIP, THE BLACK FREIGHTER
WITH THE 51 CANNONS*

OPENS FIRE ON THE TOWN

Then you gentlemen can wipe all the grins off your faces
There'll be burning in the town, there's a flap on

The whole stinking place will be down to the ground
Only this cheap hotel will be standing safe and sound

And you'll say why did they spare that one?
You'll say why did they spare that one?

Then all night through all you can do
You'll wonder who's the famous person there

And you'll see me stepping out into the morning
Looking nice, with a ribbon in my hair

*THEN THE SHIP, THE BLACK FREIGHTER
RUNS A FLAG UP THE MASTHEAD*

AND CHEERING IS HEARD

Then just before noon, there'll be hundreds of men
Pouring out of that dirty black freighter

And they're moving in the shadows, where no one can see
And they're chaining up the people
and they're bringing them to me

Asking me—kill them now or later?
Asking me—kill them now or later?

Noon on the clock, it's so still on the dock
You could hear from miles away

173

In the quiet of death i'll say--kill them now
And they'll pile up the bodies and i'll say: Hoopla!

*AND THE SHIP, THE BLACK FREIGHTER
SAILS AWAY OUT TO SEA*

AND ON IT IS ME.

DAN O'NEILL

BELFAST

UP THE FALLS ROAD IN THE BLACK TAXI FOR A PINT AT THE PRISONER'S DEPENDENTS CLUB.. WHERE I'M ASKED TO DRAW..

..A PORTRAIT OF ALLISON FOR HER HUSBAND.. HE SHOT TWO BRITISH SOLDIERS WHEN HE WAS 16 YEARS OLD.. HE DOESN'T HAVE A PICTURE OF HIS WIFE.. SO I DRAW ONE FOR HIM.. THIS HAS TO BE MY BEST DRAWING.. HE'S GOING TO BE LOOKING AT IT FOR A **LONG** TIME.. SO IT WAS.. MY VERY BEST DRAWING..

..AND NOW, IT, TOO, IS DOING A LIFE TERM IN BRITISH PRISON.. NO.. I'M NOT GOING TO REDRAW ALLISON.. ALLISON IS LIKE EVERYONE..

..ELSE IN BELFAST. YOU'LL JUST HAVE TO USE YOUR IMAGINATION..

© NEILL 85 —

174

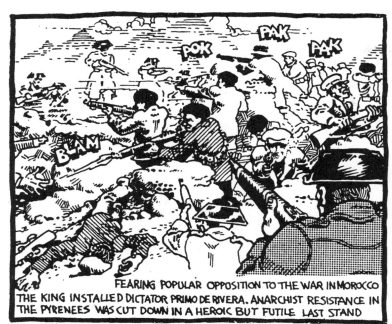

DURRUTI FLED TO CUBA WITH A FEW FRIENDS

FEARING POPULAR OPPOSITION TO THE WAR IN MOROCCO THE KING INSTALLED DICTATOR PRIMO DE RIVERA. ANARCHIST RESISTANCE IN THE PYRENEES WAS CUT DOWN IN A HEROIC BUT FUTILE LAST STAND

AT A PLANTATION WHERE THEY FOUND WORK WAGES WERE CUT. THERE WERE PROTESTS

THREE MEN WERE SEIZED, TORTURED, AND THROWN BEFORE THE WORKERS WHO WERE TOLD TO GET BACK TO THE FIELD

DURRUTI AND HIS FRIENDS DECIDED TO ACT...

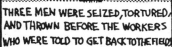

LATER, THE PLANTATION OWNER'S BODY WAS FOUND IN HIS OFFICE. A NOTE IDENTIFIED THE DEED AS "THE JUSTICE OF THE WANDERERS"

THEY, THEN, WENT TO SOUTH AMERICA WHERE THEY CARRIED OUT A SERIES OF BANK "EXPROPRIATIONS" TO FINANCE ANARCHIST PROJECTS

HIS RETURN TO EUROPE SAW YEARS OF FORCED WANDERING AND LEGAL BATTLES TO AVOID EXTRADITION

IT HAS BEEN SAID AGAINST OUR SYSTEM IN THE UKRAINE THAT IT WAS ABLE TO LAST BECAUSE IT WAS BASED ONLY ON PEASANT FORMATIONS. IT ISN'T TRUE. OUR COMMUNITIES WERE MIXED AGRICULTURAL INDUSTRIAL SOME OF THEM WERE ONLY INDUSTRIAL. WE WERE ALL OF US FIGHTERS AND WORKERS

DURING THIS TIME HE MET WITH THE GREAT UKRAINIAN ANARCHIST, NESTOR MAKHNO (SEE ANARCHY COMICS #1)

ALPHONSO XIII WAS FORCED TO ABDICATE IN 1930. AT HIS DEPARTURE FROM THE COUNTRY, A LONGSHOREMAN GAVE HIM A FITTING SEND OFF

CLASS WAR CONTINUED. THE C.N.T. AN ANARCHIST UNION TRIED SEVERAL REVOLTS BUT EACH WAS CRUSHED BY THE GOVERNMENT

178

AS THE SITUATION WORSENED, THE PEOPLE STRUCK BACK AT THE HISTORIC SYMBOL OF THEIR OPPRESSION, THE CATHOLIC CHURCH

JULY 17 1936: THE MILITARY STAGED A COUP THRU OUT SPAIN. IN BARCELONA THE UPRISING WAS CRUSHED BY ARMED WORKERS MILITIAS. THE BLOODY SPANISH CIVIL WAR HAD BEGUN

USING HOMEMADE ARMORED CARS, THE MILITIAS STOPPED FRANCO'S CRACK MOROCCAN TROOPS IN BITTER FIGHTING

King-Kong

TAK TAKTAKTAKTA

DURRUTI HELD HIS MEN TOGETHER IN THEIR ADVANCE TOWARD SARAGOSA, AS THEY ENCOUNTERED AIR ATTACKS FOR THE FIRST TIME

THE NEWLY FORMED COMMUNES OF ARAGON WERE SAFE FOR THE MOMENT BUT DANGER THREATENED IN THE SOUTH...

THE DURRUTI COLUMN MARCHED TO BELEAGUERED MADRID AND THERE PLAYED A DECISIVE ROLE IN HURLING BACK THE FASCIST INVADERS

BLAM POK

NOVEMBER 17, 1936: WHILE DIRECTING HIS TROOPS AT

CRACK

THE FRONT, DURRUTI WAS FATALLY SHOT THRU THE CHEST

AT HIS DEATH, HIS SOLE POSSESSIONS WERE AN EMPTY SUITCASE WITH A LEDGER GIVING A FULL ACCOUNT OF HIS FINANCES TO THE C.N.T.

Mark Zingarelli

the "Cockeyed" Cook STORY

© 1987 by ZINGARELLI

A Real-Life Killer Truly Born to Lose!

"I'M GONNA LIVE BY THE GUN AN' ROAM."

WILLIAM EDWARD COOK WAS BORN INTO POVERTY. WITH A GHASTLY GROWTH OVER HIS RIGHT EYE. HIS THIRD STRIKE CAME WHEN HE WAS ONLY 5 YEARS OLD...HIS FATHER DESERTED THE FAMILY AND HIS POOR MOTHER DIED A FEW MONTHS LATER.

AUTHORITIES FOUND LITTLE BILLY AND HIS SEVEN BROTHERS AND SISTERS IN A DESERTED MINE SHAFT LIVING LIKE DESPERATE, WILD ANIMALS.

FOSTER HOMES WERE HARD TO FIND FOR A KID WHO LOOKED LIKE A MONSTER, SO A KIND-HEARTED WELFARE DOCTOR OPERATED ON BILLY'S DISFIGURED FACE.

FOR THE REST OF HIS SHORT LIFE, THE HAPHAZARD SURGERY LEFT COOK WITH A HAUNTING, LEERING RIGHT EYE THAT DROOPED, SCARIN' THE BEJEEZUS OUT OF GIRLS AND PROSPECTIVE EMPLOYERS.

IT'S NO SURPRISE THAT YOUNG COOK, SPURNED AND RIDICULED BY HIS PEERS, TURNED TO PETTY CRIME. SOME SAY HE STOLE FOR NO APPARENT REASON.

SOON HE WAS LABELED 'INCORRIGIBLE' AND SENT TO A MISSOURI STATE REFORM SCHOOL FOR A YEAR.

THERE HE MET OTHER JUVIES... SOME EVEN ANGRIER THAN HIM.

HIS FIRST SENTENCE SERVED, BILLY'S OLDER SISTER CLAIMED HIM, BUT IN A FEW SHORT MONTHS HE'D CAUSED ENOUGH TROUBLE TO BE SENT BACK... THIS TIME FOR *FIVE* YEARS.

COOK'S BITTERNESS AND HATRED FOR AUTHORITY INTENSIFIED DURING THIS STRETCH AND SOME SAY ANY HOPE FOR A FUTURE AMONG 'REG'LAR FOLK' WAS DASHED.

UPON RELEASE, HE SWORE HE'D NEVER BE SENT BACK.

ON DECEMBER 30, 1950, A MOTORIST INNOCENTLY STOPS TO PICK-UP A HITCH-HIKER SOMEWHERE NEAR LUBBOCK, TEXAS.

182

WHY DON'T YOU SHUT-UP AND GET OUT OF THE CAR, ASSHOLE?

BILLY TELLS THE DRIVER THAT HE WANTS TO GO TO JOPLIN, MISSOURI—275 MILES AWAY. THE DRIVER LAUGHED, SO BILLY SHOWS HIM THE GUN AND FORCES HIM INTO THE CRAMPED REAR TRUNK.

FATE ALLOWS THE MAN TO PRY OPEN THE TRUNK AND ESCAPE. LATER, HE WILL DISCOVER JUST HOW LUCKY HE WAS.

HIS WOULD-BE VICTIM GONE, BILLY DRIVES NORTH TO ROUTE 66 WHERE HE DITCHES THE CAR. HE'S RESTLESS AND IN SEARCH OF DIFFERENT KICKS AND NEW PREY...

...HAPPEN TO FALL, 98 BOTTLES OF BEER ON THE WALL.

THE VACATIONING MOSSER FAMILY, CARL, THELMA, THEIR 3 CHILDREN AND A FAMILY DOG WERE ON THEIR WAY TO NEW MEXICO.

BILLY FLAGS DOWN THE MOSSER CAR, THEN SHOVES HIS GUN INTO CARL'S SURPRISED FACE. BILLY ORDERS CARL TO HEAD WEST.

FOR THE NEXT 24 HOURS MOSSER FOLLOWS THE GUNMAN'S AIMLESS DIRECTIONS TO CARLSBAD, NEW MEXICO, TO EL PASO, TO HOUSTON, AND FINALLY TO WICHITA FALLS, TEXAS.

YOU'RE DEAD, POPS!

AT A WICHITA FALLS FILLING STATION MOSSER TRIES TO OVERPOWER COOK, BUT FAILS...

ENRAGED, BILLY FORCES CARL TO DRIVE EAST TO JOPLIN....ON A GRAVEL SHOULDER OF A LONELY ROAD IN MISSOURI, HE SHOOTS THE ENTIRE MOSSER FAMILY AT CLOSE RANGE.

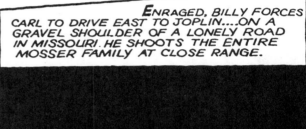

WITH THE LAST BULLET IN THE CYLINDER, HE KILLS THE DOG.

HE DUMPS THE CORPSES (OF THE FAMILY HE NEVER HAD) IN ANOTHER OLD MINE SHAFT NEAR HIS CHILDHOOD HOME.

COOK ABANDONS THE MOSSER CAR AND HEADS WEST AGAIN... A GUN IN HIS BELT MAKES ANYTHING SEEM POSSIBLE.

MEANWHILE...ON JANUARY 3, 1951, A SHERIFF DISCOVERS THE BULLET-RIDDLED AND BLOOD-STAINED CAR. HE TRACES IT TO CARL MOSSER.

NEXT, THE GAS STATION ATTENDANT IN WICHITA FALLS RECOUNTS THE MOSSER-COOK STRUGGLE FOR THE LOCAL POLICE.

THE GUNMAN'S DESCRIPTION IS FURTHER CORROBORATED BY A MOTORIST WHO FLED FROM HIS STOLEN CAR'S TRUNK.

AND WHEN HIS CAR IS RECOVERED, A CRUMPLED RECEIPT FOR A HANDGUN PURCHASED IN EL PASO IS ALSO FOUND. IT'S MADE OUT TO W.E. COOK.

INTERSTATE POLICE RECORDS ARE CHECKED AND THE MANHUNT FOR WILLIAM E. COOK BEGINS!

THE TRAIL LEADS TO BLYTHE, CALIFORNIA — CLOSE TO THE ARIZONA BORDER.

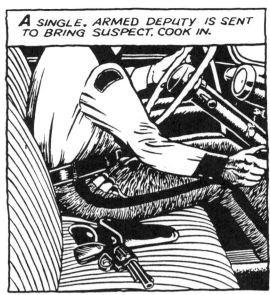

A SINGLE, ARMED DEPUTY IS SENT TO BRING SUSPECT, COOK IN.

THE LUCKLESS OFFICER UNDERESTIMATES COOK AND FINDS HIMSELF ON THE WRONG END OF BILLY'S GUN.

BILLY FORCES HIM TO DRIVE HIS CAR DEEP INTO THE DESERT.

AMAZINGLY, BILLY LEAVES HIM ALONE & UNHARMED ON AN ISOLATED BUTTE.

THE CRUISER IS FAR TOO HOT AND EASY TO TRACE SO BILLY ABANDONS IT JUST OUTSIDE YUMA, ARIZONA.

LATER THAT DAY, HE WILL FORCE HIMSELF ON YET ANOTHER HAPLESS MOTORIST...NAMED ROBERT DEWEY.

WITHOUT A SECOND THOUGHT, BILLY SHOOTS DEWEY IN THE CHEST AND THROWS HIM INTO THE MIDDLE OF THE ROAD. DEWEY IS DEAD BEFORE HE HITS THE PAVEMENT...

WORRIED, BUT THRILLED BY THE CLOSING DRAGNET, BILLY COOK HEADS SOUTH INTO MEXICO WITH A VAGUE PLAN TO BUY A WOMAN AND SMUGGLE HER BACK INTO THE STATES...

RELENTLESSLY TRACKED, COOK IS FINALLY ARRESTED IN MEXICO WITHOUT A STRUGGLE. AND HE HAS ALREADY THOUGHT OF A CLEVER STORY...

JESUS CHRIST! ALL I REMEMBER IS...UH...GETTING *REALLY* LOADED A FEW DAYS BEFORE CHRISTMAS...SHIT... THE *NEXT* THING I REMEMBER IS...UH...WAKING UP IN A MEX *WHOREHOUSE!*

WILLIAM COOK WAS TRIED FOR THE MURDER OF ROBERT DEWEY, FOUND GUILTY, AND SENT TO SAN QUENTIN PRISON TO AWAIT SENTENCING.

EVENTUALLY, THE REMAINS OF THE MOSSER FAMILY WERE FOUND IN THAT FORSAKEN MINE SHAFT NEAR JOPLIN. THEIR DEATHS WERE ATTRIBUTED TO COOK...

ON DECEMBER 12, 1952, COOK DIED IN THE SAN QUENTIN GAS CHAMBER... DEFIANT AND BITTER TO THE END, HIS FINAL WORDS BESPOKE THE DARKNESS OF HIS SOUL.

I HATE EVERYBODY'S GUTS!

End

DENNIS THE SULLEN MENACE

BY DENNIS P. EICHHORN AND MICHAEL DOUGAN

A FEW YEARS AGO I GOT BUSTED FOR DEALING ACID AND MARIJUANA.

THE JUDGE GAVE ME THREE YEARS IN THE IDAHO STATE PENITENTIARY.

IN IDAHO, FIRST TIME OFFENDERS CAN GET OUT IN FOUR MONTHS IF THEY DON'T FUCK UP. THE OTHER CONVICTS CALLED US "120 DAY RIDERS."

THE NEW ARRIVALS WERE KEPT SEPARATE FROM THE REST OF THE PRISON POPULATION IN A CELL CALLED "THE FISHTANK." WE WERE THE FISH.

WE ATE SEPARATELY FROM THE OTHER CONVICTS. AS I STOOD IN LINE WAITING FOR MY FIRST MEAL I NOTICED A MEXICAN IN A WHITE WAITER'S JACKET WALKING TOWARD ME...

AS HE CAME ALONGSIDE ME HE WHIRLED AND STABBED THE GUY IN FRONT OF ME IN THE BACK

THE GUY FELL TO THE FLOOR SCREAMING IN PAIN. IN A MATTER OF MINUTES, HE WAS DEAD.

AAAAAAAAAAAAAUGH!!

THE GUARDS TOOK US ALL TO SEPARATE CELLS AND QUESTIONED US. I KNEW ENOUGH TO SAY I HADN'T SEEN ANYTHING.

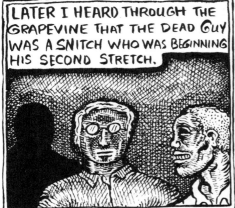

LATER I HEARD THROUGH THE GRAPEVINE THAT THE DEAD GUY WAS A SNITCH WHO WAS BEGINNING HIS SECOND STRETCH.

SOME PEOPLE HAD BEEN WAITING FOR YEARS TO GET HIM. I ALSO LEARNED THAT IT ONLY COST TWO CARTONS OF CIGARETTES TO HAVE SOMEONE KILLED.

FOLDING MONEY WASN'T ALLOWED BEHIND THE WALLS AND CIGARETTES WERE THE MEDIUM OF EXCHANGE. SOME PEOPLE HAD HUNDREDS OF CARTONS STACKED UNDER THEIR BUNKS.

AFTER **3** WEEKS, I WAS MOVED TO A MEDIUM SECURITY WORKFARM IN THE NEARBY DESERT

THE PRISONERS WERE NEARLY ALL FIRST-TIMERS, LIKE MYSELF, OR LIFERS WHO HAD BEEN LOCKED UP FOR YEARS. MOST OF THE GUARDS WERE MORMONS

EVERYONE BUT ME WAS TATTOOED. MY CELLMATE, WHO WAS DOING 30 YEARS, HAD A DEVIL'S HEAD TATTOO ON HIS INNER LEFT ELBOW.

HE HAD A THREE-CARTON A DAY SMACK HABIT. EVERY NIGHT, I'D WATCH AS HE SHOT HIMSELF UP...

WHY DO YOU ALWAYS HIT UP IN THE DEVIL'S FACE?

UUUH!

OVER THE YEARS, HIS TATTOO HAD BECOME...BLUISH SCAR TISSUE...

IT FEELS RIGHT...

DURING THE DAYS, I WORKED OUTSIDE. MY JOB WAS TO WALK ACROSS NEWLY-HARROWED FIELDS TOSSING ROCKS INTO A SLOW-MOVING DUMPTRUCK.

188

THE WORK WAS INCREDIBLY BORING. TO PASS THE TIME I MADE UP SONGS AND PLAYED IMAGINARY GAMES WITH ROCKS

ALICE

BETTY.

CHRISTY

DENISE

SOMETIMES I PLAYED MENTAL MONOPOLY. I FOUND THAT I COULD REMEMBER EVERY DETAIL OF THE GAME.

7....LET'S SEE...

THAT PUTS ME ON......CHANCE....

OKAY, PICK A CARD...

GO TO JAIL!

HAHAHAHA!!! JAIL!. HAHAHAHA... DO NOT PASS GO HAHAHA..

ONE DAY, ANOTHER CONVICT FLIPPED OUT AND TRIED TO KILL ME BY THROWING A LARGE ROCK AT ME.

IT NARROWLY MISSED MY HEAD.

WHOOPS HAHAHA...

I NEVER TURNED MY BACK TO HIM AFTER THAT

I KNEW WHERE HE WAS EVERY HOUR OF THE DAY. EVEN IN MY SLEEP I KNEW EXACTLY WHERE HE WAS....

dennis eichhorn & michael dougan

NIGHTS WERE THE WORST. SOMETIMES THERE WOULD BE A RAPE OR GANG BANG. I KNEW ENOUGH TO SAY I HADN'T HEARD ANYTHING...

TAKE IT PUNK!

HUH?

HAHAHAHAHAHAHA

IT DIDN'T TAKE ME LONG TO DEVELOP AN AIR OF SULLEN MENACE. I DIDN'T HAVE MUCH TO SAY TO ANYONE. THAT WAS NOTHING UNUSUAL. A LOT OF PEOPLE "DUMMIED UP."

NO! GET AWAY FROM ME! AAA AAAAAUGH!

SOMETIMES AFTER DINNER I'D SIT IN THE CAFETERIA AND PLAY CHESS WITH A MURDERER FROM POCATELLO.

YOUR MOVE

ONE EVENING, A BIG PSYCHOTIC NAMED KERMIT KIBITZED OUR GAME.

189

KERMIT WAS A BASQUE FROM IDAHO FALLS.

HE'D RAPED AND KILLED A WOMAN AND EATEN OF HER FLESH.

THE GUARDS KEPT KERMIT HEAVILY TRANQUILIZED AND WATCHED HIM CLOSELY.

I WON THE GAME I WAS PLAYING.

PLAY ME

...ALL RIGHT

I USED THE FOOL'S CHECKMATE AND BEAT KERMIT IN FOUR MOVES.

KERMIT PICKED UP MY QUEEN

SNAP

THE GUARD BEHIND HIM STEPPED CLOSER

SORRY. I'll FIX IT...

THE NEXT EVENING, KERMIT APPEARED AFTER SUPPER. HE SILENTLY HANDED ME THE REPAIRED QUEEN.

KERMIT HAD USED SO MUCH EPOXY, THE CHESS-PIECE WAS COMPLETELY ENCASED IN A GLOB OF CLEAR PLASTIC.

THANKS.

NO PROBLEM.

190

THERE'S A GOOD SHOW ON T.V. TONIGHT, YOU CAN COME AND WATCH IT WITH US IN THE LIFERS' LOUNGE

THE LIFERS' LOUNGE WAS A RECREATION ROOM RESERVED FOR THE KILLER ELITE.

TO SAY "NO THANKS" WOULD BE A DEADLY INSULT.

SOUNDS GOOD

SEE YOU AT NINE

AT NINE O'CLOCK I WENT TO THE LIFERS' LOUNGE...

... DICKIE, IDAHO'S MOST INFAMOUS MASS MURDERER WAS ADJUSTING THE KNOBS.

THE T.V. MOVIE OF THE WEEK WAS TRUMAN CAPOTE'S ...: "IN COLD BLOOD." I TOOK A SEAT NEAR THE BACK AND TRIED TO MAKE MYSELF INVISIBLE.

IT'S A SURE THING DICKIE!

THE LIFERS WATCHED INTENTLY AS PERRY AND DICK SLAUGHTERED...

LOOK AT ME BOY...'CAUSE I'M THE LAST LIVING THING YOU'RE GONNA SEE ...

PLEASE DON'T HURT US...

POW!

... THE CLUTTER FAMILY AND WENT ON THE RUN...

40 DOLLARS!

DON'T TAKE THE RADIO!

DON'T HURT THE CHILDREN

LEAVE THE BINOCULARS!

POW!

THE LIFERS WERE ROOTING FOR THE KILLERS.

BURN THE BOOTS!!!

DUMBFUCK

191

WHEN DICK AND PERRY WERE FINGERED BY FLOYD. THE LIFERS WERE INCENSED.

YOU LEFT THESE FOOTPRINTS IN THE CLUTTER'S BLOOD, AND A LIVING WITNESS!

FUCKING SNITCH!

PERRY'S HANGING QUIETED THE LIFERS DOWN.

SIGH.

ONE BY ONE THEY LEFT THE LOUNGE, WRAPPED IN THEIR OWN THOUGHTS. I WAS LEFT ALONE.

I TURNED OFF THE SET AND WENT TO MY CELL.

I DIDN'T SLEEP TOO WELL THAT NIGHT.

193

TRANSLATED BY: ELIZABETH BELL   LETTERED BY: LEA HERNANDEZ   Muñoz et Sampayo.

194

Marti (ribera)

THE LAW

--EVERY SATURDAY, I'VE GOT TO CLEAN UP THIS MESS. THE COUNTRY'S A SHAMBLES! IT'S A HELL OF A JOB.

--THE LAW SAYS TO THE STATE:

--YOU DISGUSTING SLOB, YOU'VE LEFT THE COUNTRY A TOTAL WRECK.

THIEVES, HARLOTS, PISSANTS, SWINDLERS, PERVERTS, TERRORISTS, RAPISTS...THE WHOLE BIT!...

THE STATE DOESN'T TAKE IT LYING DOWN

--YEAH, I SUPPOSE YOU THINK YOU COULD GET RID OF ALL THIS SHIT...

--ALWAYS THE SAME, STATE. -I'M FED UP WITH PLAYING JANITOR FOR YOUR DECADENCE!

--WHATCHA GONNA DO-- REBEL?

--GOD FORBID! IF I REBEL, THE WHOLE THING'S DOWN THE TUBES.

--IF ONLY... YOU KNOW DAMN WELL... IF YOU'D LET ME USE **EVERYTHING** I'VE GOT...

HERE COMES THE SPOILSPORT.

--STOP RIGHT THERE, LAW! PUT ON THE BRAKES!

TRANSLATED BY: ELIZABETH BELL   LETTERED BY: LEAHERNANDEZ

197

COLIN UPTON
STALINGRAD

YOU...? ARE ALL THE RUSSIANS.?

HA! THOSE PEASANTS?! HARDLY! I'M WITH HELL'S RUSSIAN EXPEDITIONARY FORCE ACCORDING TO THE PACT BETWEEN STALIN AND SATAN.

STALIN WAS DESPERATE! THE WESTERN ALLIES REFUSED TO OPEN THE 2ND FRONT EVEN AS THE RED ARMY SUFFERED MASSIVE LOSSES. HE NEEDED SOLDIERS SO HE CAME CRAWLING TO US. SATAN FOUND THIS ALL QUITE AMUSING.

NOT EVEN OUR POOR SOVIET COMRADES KNOW WHO WE ARE, EXCEPT FOR A FEW HIGH-RANKING KOMMISARS. WE HAVE OUR OWN UNITS OR MIX IN ANONYMOUSLY WITH THE CONSCRIPTS WHEN NEW DIVISIONS ARE FORMED. WE OFTEN ARE PROMOTED FOR OUR COURAGE.

200

OF COURSE, IT'S EASY TO BE BRAVE. YOU KILL OUR EARTHY BODIES AND WE SIMPLY GO BACK TO HELL TO ACQUIRE A NEW ONE, WE DON'T CARE!!

BUT WHY DO YOU DO THIS?

SOULS! NICE JUICY SOULS! MILLIONS OF THEM! ALL SUPPLIED BY STALIN IN THE INTEREST OF THE STATE — A FEW GOOD MASSACRES AND POGRAMS, WE SHOULD DO NICELY!!

PLUS WE LOVE A GOOD FIGHT! I MUST BE GOING BEFORE THEY COME LOOKING FOR ME.

YOU'RE NOT GOING TO KILL ME?

DON'T BE SILLY, I ENJOYED CHATTING WITH YOU. YOUR MEN ARE OVER THERE.

FAREWELL AND BE GONE!

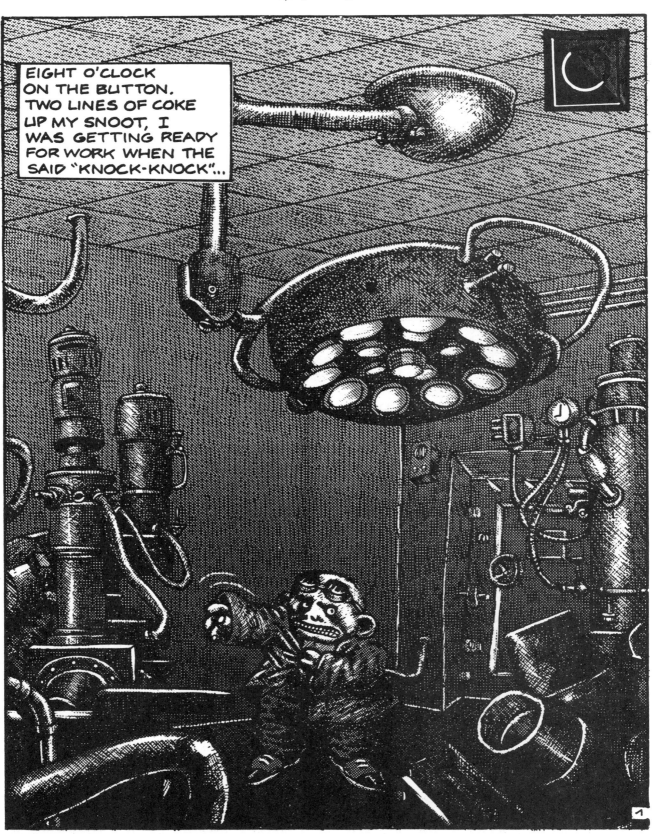

EIGHT O'CLOCK ON THE BUTTON. TWO LINES OF COKE UP MY SNOOT, I WAS GETTING READY FOR WORK WHEN THE SAID "KNOCK-KNOCK"...

TRANSLATED BY: ELIZABETH BELL
LETTERED BY: LEA HERNANDEZ

THE TWO POLICE GOONS STANDING IN MY HALLWAY ASKED WHERE MY TICKET WAS...

ONE CATCH. I DIDN'T HAVE A TICKET. NEVER EVEN HEARD OF ANY GODDAM TICKET... BEFORE THEY LEFT, THE TWO COPS INFORMED ME THAT IF I DIDN'T HAVE IT THE NEXT MORNING THEY'D TAKE ME AWAY...

2

WHEN I GOT TO THE FACTORY, I EXPLAINED TO THE FOREMAN. THE BASTARD TOOK THE OPPORTUNITY TO KICK ME OFF THE JOB.

204

FOR BUREAUCRATIC DOCUMENTZ, LIKE TICKETZ, GO TO A BUREAU. SO I RUSHED OVER TO CENTRAL ADMINISTRATION.

AFTER AN ENDLESS WAIT IN LINE, I WAS TOLD IN RANK BREATH THAT NO TICKETZ HAD BEEN ISSUED FOR SOME TIME...

MY MORALE AT SUB-ZERO, I DECIDED TO LOOK FOR MY ONLY FRIEND AT THE CANTEEN. THE MENU: RAT STEAK, FAKE GRAVY. SUBLIMELY REVOLTING...

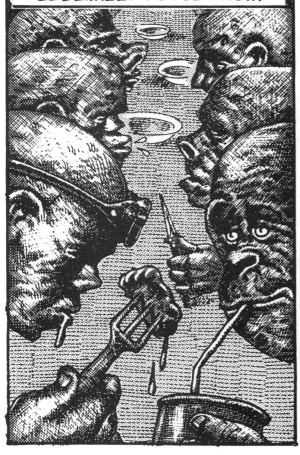

GETTING RIGHT DOWN TO BUSINESS, I ASKED HIM TO LEND ME HIS TICKET. HE REFUSED FLAT OUT. I STUCK MY FORK BETWEEN HIS EYES, GRABBED THE PRECIOUS THING, AND FLED.

4

EVEN WITH THE DOOR HEAVILY LOCKED...

I WAS PARANOID...

UNTIL MORNING CAME...

AT EIGHT ON THE BUTTON, WHEN THE DOOR SAID "KNOCK-KNOCK" AGAIN, I RUSHED TO OPEN IT, BEAMING, THE TICKET IN MY HAND...

THE MURDERER OF HUNG

STORY: DOMINIQUE GRANGE   ART: TARDI

Nguyen Thi Loan was one of the boat people, an escapee from the wars in Vietnam and other horrors.

She had been in New York for eight months, and had managed to get herself a job, although her papers were not in order.

She worked in a restaurant in Chinatown, owned by Vietnamese immigrants who had fled when the French first unleashed fear and death on their country.

Late again, Loan! You should go to bed earlier so you can get here on time. If you do it again...

Loan felt the manageress didn't like her, but made the best of it. She thought of her father, an active FNL militant from the start, who chose to stay behind despite the poverty and repression. He must have thought accepting better than fleeing, after his life of combat...

She thought of Jerzy from the flat next door. He had become a close friend, the only one who knew why she had come all the way to New York...

Jerzy! Any news?

They say at the Rialto they haven't seen BRIXTON since he took off without paying.

The Rialto's a run-down flophouse full of one year tenants living in ten-foot boxes. If he can't even afford that, then he sure has sunk pretty low!

Since we've been after that brute, his trail leads down and down. I never knew there were so many hotels and slums full of sleaze, rats, roaches and every kind of filth in New York. How can they get to sleep in all that shit?

I won't hold it against you if you want to give up Jerzy. You've helped me so much already. If you like, I could carry on the search alone. We'd still be friends.

But Jerzy didn't give up. Loan was his friend. While she was at work, he continued his investigations. He was retired and besides a little part time maintenance work in the block, he could spend his time as he liked.

What do you want?

I'm looking for Slim ANDERSON.

Slim don't live here no more. He's gone to Brooklyn. You a friend of his?

The woman gave him Slim's work address. Whenever she had time off, Loan dedicated herself to her one goal: finding Cliff BRIXTON. Jerzy always came with her.

Slim ANDERSON?

What do you want with Slim ANDERSON?

It's personal... about one of his friends.

I'm ANDERSON. Now what do you want?

Well, I'm looking for an old buddy I've lost track of. I've been told you worked with him in Atlantic City. His name's CLIFF BRIXTON.

Any idea what happened to him?

I kinda knew BRIXTON. He was real moody, sometimes he wouldn't speak to no-one for days at a time. We worked on maintenance at the Casino for three years... But I never figured him out. He was a real weirdo, a loner.

211

One day he just told me he couldn't handle Atlantic City no more. All that glitter, the gamblers, the dough... an' the old hookers hanging around the docks, looking for pick ups... It blew his head... You'd never see him with a girl. He said he'd found a service station job on South Street. That's the last I heard of him.

Patiently, methodically, they rang up all the service stations on the East Side. They worked through the list with scrupulous care, confident that they would suceed.

Sometimes I wonder why you're doing this for me, Jerzy? You're old enough to be my father...

How can I explain how close I feel to her? Me, Jerzy KUPINSKY, a polish immigrant. I've also lived with the loneliness of this city since the War... and like Loan, I'm not afraid. We've both lived through terror, the horrors of war in our own countries, before coming to New York. Compared to all that, life here seems almost comforting.

Jerzy, you're very quiet?

I was thinking about that evening in july when we went up on the tenement roof for some air...

...The Americans had already destroyed part of the village where I was a school teacher. Most of the men were out fighting. Only the old, the sick and the children were left. I lived alone with my son. His father had been killed in the bombing when I was six months pregnant.

212

I was rushing around, trying to save some of those defenseless people. Everyone was fleeing from the village, trying to get to the shelters.

Suddenly I remembered a young pregnant woman who was about to give birth. I hadn't seen her among the evacuees..

...I went back through the village with Hung, my four year old son.

That was just the beginning...

I tried to get to the shelter...

...I could hear the screams of the animals massacred by the Marines, who were cleaning up the place...stealing the little we had left and firing at anything that still moved...

Suddenly..

HEY, YOU THERE! HOLD IT!

I knew he was going to kill us. But I begged him to spare my son.

He made us go into one of the houses that were still standing and there he raped me in front of my child. Hung kept crying and calling out, "Mummy are you hurt?" Suddenly he came up and started hitting the American with his little hand.

...Then the Marine grabbed Hung, made him stand against the wall, and shot him in the back. He was crazy. He put the gun to my head, but... I don't know why... He let me live...

He just walked off without a word. I lay there for several hours, I couldn't even get over to my child's body. When the people came back to the village they found his wallet nearby. It must have dropped out of his pocket. It had some photos in it...

214

This is my only lead.

"The whole BRIXTON family in front of the shop!" Mom-Cliff-Dad (NYC-june 1968)

I've come to New York to find the murderer of Hung.

For seven months, they patiently worked at their investigations. The last piece of information took them to a sleazy bar in the Bowery, where BRIXTON, now a terminal alcoholic, was said to spend whole days at a time

Loan had a revolver in her pocket and her finger was curled round the trigger. But her face was calm and she felt quite determined. Jerzy asked about BRIXTON.

He's on the side-walk across the street, taking his bottle for a walk! HAH! HA! HAH!

And Loan saw him, again. He had left his left leg in Vietnam and the war had turned him into an alcoholic. He had sunken lower and lower...

...down into the Bowery gutter. The man who thought he'd got away with murdering Hung and raping Loan, the swaggering Marine, was now a total wreck.. terrible memories came flooding back to the young woman's mind, but Jerzy brought her back to reality.

Give me my revolver, Loan.

You don't need it now. Life has taken revenge on him for you. Come on, there's nothing left to do here...

WINES LIQUORS

FIN

215

the great literary successes of the new comics movement have come, largely, in the field of biographical and auto-biographical writing. not accidentally, most of the more talented women comic strip artists have chosen to work in this area of the field. it was harvey pekar of cleveland, ohio, in his regular comics magazine **american splendor**, who first mastered the contours of the new graphic short story. along with art spiegelman's **maus**, pekar's **american splendor** short stories remain the new comics movement's finest literary achievement to date.

Lendor

the forthcoming

American Splendor

218 SUPPER TIME
by Will Eisner

The soul of the old working class, ethnic neighborhoods of America is brilliantly revealed in this beautiful epiphany by the spiritual father of the New Comics movement.

220 GROWING UP AS ARNIE'S GIRL
by Aline Kominsky

The world of a second generation Jewish American "Princess" is turned inside out by the Roseanne Barr of the New Comics movement.

225 BINKY BROWN IN "THE TABOO GOWN"
by Justin Green

The creator of the now immortal "Binky Brown meets the Blessed Virgin Mary" spins a new, guilt drenched, 1950s Irish Catholic Binky tale.

227 MOONSHINE MAMA
by Lee Marrs

Berkeley's Lee Marrs spins a wonderful "back to 'bama" tale.

231 MIDWESTERN WEDDING
by Carol Lay

Surrealism is ultimately at issue in this "almost entirely true" voyage back to the old home town by Los Angeles artist, and comic strip experimentalist, Carol Lay.

236 THE WHISPERING TREE
by Gilbert Hernandez

The mythical Mexican village of Palomar, and its traditions, becomes the central character in this modern folk tale by the co-author of *Love & Rockets*.

239 THE GOAT
by Jaime Hernandez

A slice of life from Maggie's world — the world of contemporary, working class Los Angeles — is deftly rendered by the other co-author of *Love & Rockets*.

240 LABOR
by Carol Tyler

The weight of life for two generations of working class women is captured in this wonderful, multi-layered story.

244 FUNSLOWER FEEDS
by Mario Hernandez

A daydream becomes a binding pack between the generations in this charming reverie by the San Francisco branch of Los Bro Hernandez.

245 IT'S VERY HARD TO FIND HER AT NIGHT
by Jayr Pulga

The contrapuntal use of graphic image and narrative line open up a whole new series of possibilities for New Comics writing in this pioneering story.

248 THE DREAM BOOK BUSINESS
by Ben Katchor

One of the best stories so far in Katchor's unfolding literary delineation of daily life in the old Jewish ethnic neighborhoods south of Delancey Street in New York City.

253 DAPPER JOHN MINDS THE BABY
by Eddie Campbell

For Scotland's Eddie Campbell, parenthood has changed just about everything for the regulars back in the days of the Ace Rock N' Roll Club.

260 HOW MY FAMILY ENCOURAGED ME TO BECOME AN ARTIST
by Dori Seda

A rich sense of detail and texture, and a winning sense of humor, carry forward this two-page minor epic by the late Dori Seda, the most talented and popular New Comics artist of her generation.

262 50 YEARS AGO (THE ADVENTURES OF HERGE)
by Joost Swarte

The genius of Herge — the creator of Tin Tin — is paid proper homage in this now classic tale by the great Joost Swarte, Herge's true heir, and the dean of the European "Clear Line" school of New Comics literature.

265 PATTON
by R. Crumb

The life and times of the brilliant Mississippi delta blues singer retold by the greatest American comic strip artist of the modern era.

277 WHAT BIG GIRLS ARE MADE OF
by Dianne Noomin

The editor of *Twisted Sisters*, and the creator of that showgirl shopping hound, Didi Glitz, reveals the exact tension point where the New Comics turn into a poem.

279 HYPOTHETICAL QUANDARY
by Harvey Pekar. Art by R. Crumb

Two of the medium's most talented artists collaborate on a true masterpiece of New Comics literature.

Lee Marrs

MOONSHINE MAMA

A BLEND OF TRUE-LIFE DOWNHOME TALES © 1976 BY 'BAMA CHILE LEE MARRS—

WHY, JOYCE! HALLO CHILE!

HEY, GRANDMA! I HAD TO GET AWAY FOR A REST!

SKREE

...SO MUCH HASSLE AT THE CO-OP. I GET REALLY TIRED. AND MOM'S ON THAT GET-MARRIED KICK AGAIN. SHE NEVER GIVES UP.

OH, YOUR MOM NEVER HAD A LICK O' SENSE. IT'S GOOD, YOU LEARNIN' TO GET ALONG. PLENTY OF TIME FOR MARRIAGE.

WELL, I'VE NEVER KNOWN YOU AND MOM TO AGREE ON ANYTHING ANYWAY. YOU MARRIED EARLY THOUGH, DIDN'T YOU? THEN GRANDPA BEN DIED... SAY, HOW DID YOU GET ALONG BY YOURSELF?

OH, THE SAME AS ALWAYS.

I WUZ TRAINED EARLY IN THE BREWIN' OF WHITE LIGHTNIN'.

I USED TO HELP MY PAPA 'CAUSE THERE WUZ NO SONS. I WUZ THE OLDEST, SO I LEARNED THE TRADE.

MORE PEELIN'S, ALICE.

MOONSHINER! WOW!

IT WUZ NICE. RIDIN' THE HILLS AT NIGHT WITH PAPA... MAKIN' DELIVERY.

BLAM BLAM

HMM.. GOLDURN REVENOOERS. GIT DOWN ALICE!

THAT MUST HAVE BEEN EXCITING.

OH, NAW, MOSTLY JUST HARD WORK. GATHERIN' WOOD, TENDIN' THE BREW, SMELLIN' JUST LIKE TURPENTINE ALL THE LIVELONG DAY. AND THE CHIGGERS! BUT WE MADE THE BEST BREW IN SEVEN COUNTIES.

THEM COAL OPERATOR OWNERS THOUGHT THEY OWNED US ALL. AND THEIR DEPUTIES WUZ SURE THAT WE WUZ NUTHIN' BUT DIRT.

WE KNOW YOUR MAN IS A STRIKER, LADY. NOW, WHERE IS HE?

BEN OFTEN HAD TO HIDE IN THE WOODS. THEY WOULD HAVE SHOT 'IM.

WHERE IS HE?

AS IT WUZ, THE MINE GOT BEN — HE CAME DOWN WITH THE BLACK LUNG. IT CAME ON HIM GRADUAL, BUT FINALLY IT LAID HIM FLAT FOR SURE.

SO, THEN I STARTED TO PUT MY OAR IN AGIN. POOR BEN COULDN'T WORK. I DID.

WITH PISTOLS AND WITH RIFLES, THEY TAKE AWAY OUR BREAD, AND IF YOU MINERS HINTED IT, THEY'LL SOCK YOU ON THE HEAD! WHICH SIDE ARE YOU ON? WHICH SIDE ARE YOU ON?

FIRST, I STARTED IN TO RUNNIN' THE STILL ONCET MORE. WE ALL HAD TO EAT, YA KNOW. BEN COULDN'T HARDLY GET AROUND.

THAS FINE, LIL' BEN. NOW PUT ON SOME MORE PEELIN'S HEAH.

THEN, THAT SPRING, THE LORD TOOK BEN FROM ME.

THEY'LL PAY FOR THIS, BEN! I SWEAR IT!

AFTER THAT I HAD TO MOVE AROUND MOST ALL THE TIME.

O'ER IN HARLAN HOLLOW, WE'RE GETTIN' TREATED THE SAME — LIKE DIRT. THE OPERATORS ONLY LISTEN IF WE STRIKE. ARE YOU WITH US?

IT'S ALICE, THE ROVIN' PICKET...

WELL, THAT'S WHEN I HAD TO GIVE OVER YOUR MAMA AND UNCLES TO AUNT MELISSA. YOUR MAMA, SHE NEVER DID FORGIVE ME FOR THAT. I COULDN'T EVER MAKE IT UP TO HER...

SO, YOU RASCAL, YOU'VE MADE MOONSHINE ALL YOUR LIFE?

OH, LAN' SAKES, NO, DEAH.

ONCET I WUZ MARRIED GRANPA BEN WOULD NOT HEAR OF MY WORKIN'... OUTSIDE.

AH, THE USUAL

WELL, IT HAD BEEN HARD AFTER PAPA DIED. I WUZ 11 YRS OF AGE, BUT STRONG. SO I RAN THE STILL. AND...

OOOH SUSSANNAH OOOH DONT YEWW CRY..

GOT TO KNOW ALL THE ROADS HEREABOUTS. MY, BUT I LOVED TO DRIVE THAT TRUCK. THERE WERE FUN TIMES NOW & AGIN.

LOST HIM AGAIN, DAMMIT!

THEN I MET BEN. I WUZ ONLY 14 YEARS OF AGE. SKINNY AS A RAIL—TWICE AS SHARP.

BUT BEN, HE SAID I WUZ THE WARMEST BAG O' BONES IN THESE HEAH HILLS.

229

TIMES GOT EVEN HARDER THEN, WHAT WITH THE CHILLUN COMIN' ON SO FAST. I HAD MY HANDS FULL. BEN WUZ STILL GOIN' DOWN TO THE MINES, LIKE HE HAD SINCE HE WUZ NINE. EVERY DAWN I'D SEE HIM GO AND WONDER IF HE'D COME ON HOME ALIVE. EVERY DAY TWO OR THREE WUZ CRIPPLED OR KILT.

THE MENFOLK BEGAN MEETIN' ABOUT NO SAFETY, WAGES BEIN' HELD OVER... PRICES IN THE COMPANY STORE GOIN' UP. GRIEVANCES..

THE COAL OPERATORS DIDN'T TAKE TO THAT. THEY WANTED IT ALL TO STAY THE SAME. SO THEY UP AND HIRED THEMSELVES SOME "DEPUTIES".

IT'S THEM GUN THUGS!

I DIDN'T LIKE THAT TRAVELIN'...

IT'S THE GUN THUGS!

QUICK, ALICE, YO YOU KNOW THE ROAD!

OVER THREE COUNTIES WE MOVED. IT WUZ YEARS 'FORE I LIT IN ONE PLACE TO STAY.

WE'RE SAFE! YOU BARNEY OLDFIELD!

BUT THEM WUZ CLOSE TIMES TOO. PEOPLE HELPED EACH OTHER OUT. WE SHARED LOTS MORE THEN THAN NOW.

WE'RE TEARIN' UP AN OLE RECIPE OF POVERTY AND WAR.. WE DON'T KNOW WHY WE'RE HUNGRY, NOR WHAT WE'RE FIGHTIN' FER..

230

AN COMPANY STORE

COFFEE

SORRY, SAM, BUT WE GOTTA HAVE FOOD FOR THE CHILLUN.

DRINK ORANGE JU

EVEN SO, WE HAD TO DO A FEW THINGS WE'D RATHER NOT HAVE DONE.

...TO FEED THEM CHILLUN WE... OH, LOOK AT THE TIME! YOU GET TO BED, YOUNG LADY. I'VE JUST GUMMED THE NIGHT AWAY! YOU SILLY BUNNY.

NEXT DAY:

OOOH GRANDMA!

NOW, NOW, YOU DON'T EAT RIGHT! THESE'LL JUST TIDE YOU OVER..

NEXT TIME I'LL STAY LONGER, BUT I'VE GOT TO GO OVER THE CO-OP MONTHLY BILLS BY MONDAY.

YOU TAKE CARE NOW, Y'HEAH? DON'T WORK SO HARD, HONEY CHILE.

PAT PAT

EVEN ONE NIGHT HERE MAKES ME APPRECIATE THE COLOR OF MY OWN LIFE. POOR GRANDMA... LIVED IN THESE HILLS HER WHOLE LIFE... SUCH A DRAB, HARD TIME SHE'S HAD... NOW SHE'S STUCK UP HERE..ALONE. CHEEZ, CAN'T WAIT TO GET BACK TO THE CO-OP! STILL.. A ONETIME MOONSHINER. PRETTY HEAVY. AT LEAST SHE'S GOT MEMORIES.

TOO BAD ABOUT JOYCE. SUCH A HARDWORKIN', SOLEMN LIFE SHE LEADS. BETCHA SHE HASN'T GIGGLED IN YEARS. OH WELL. HMM. PRETTY GOOD BATCH OF BREW.. MEBBE I'LL TAKE A JAR OVER TO OL' HARRY'S PLACE AFTER TONIGHT'S UNION MEETIN'...SLURP-SLURP.

END

THEY ALL DRESS UP EXCEPT FOR MRS. BREWSER WHO FIXES BREAKFAST FOR EVERYBODY. THEN THEY LEAVE FOR THE WEDDING AND MR. LLOYD GETS LOST ON THE FREEWAY AGAIN...

OKAY, WE'LL GO REAL SLOW NOW. SURE YOU DON'T WANT ME TO DRIVE?

FORTUNATELY, THEY CONTINUE ON IN SEPARATE CARS...

WHY'S SHE WEARING PANTS TO HER DAUGHTER'S WEDDING? I THOUGHT SHE WAS A REAL CONSERVATIVE TYPE.

G.I. WAR BRIDES

SHE'S GOT TO WORK AFTER THE RECEPTION.

...PAST LE SEUR'S GREEN GIANT AND DOZENS OF SNOW-COVERED FARMS...

HOW COME THE WEDDING IS SO FAR OUT IN THE STICKS?

AND WHY ARE THOSE PEOPLE SO BITTER?

THEY USED TO PUBLISH A PAPER OUT HERE BUT THEY WENT BANKRUPT...

AS THEY FINALLY APPROACH THE LITTLE TOWN WHICH THE BREWSERS CALL "HOME" CORA EYES A MIDWESTERN ARCHITECTURAL NOVELTY...

THE NUMBER OF THE BEAST IS 666 AND HE IS AMONG US.

WOW!

...AND AROUND THE BEND...

CUTE CHURCH.

WE'RE VERY EARLY... THE CEREMONY DOESN'T START FOR AN HOUR AND A HALF. I SUPPOSE WE'LL ALL GET TO KNOW THE BREWSERS BETTER.

233

AFTER EVERYONE RUNS OUT OF THINGS TO DO, JUNIOR FINDS SOMETHING TO FILL TIME WITH-- THE PLOT OF HIS INVENTIVE GHOST STORY...

IT WAS ABOUT A GUY WHO TAKES A LOT OF--

--DRUGS AND THIS OTHER GUY FLIES AWAY AFTER HE EATS THE DRUGGED GUY'S EYEBALL, BUT HE BARFS IT UP AND SO HE LICKS UP THE BARF AND...

JUNIOR, I DON'T THINK YOU'D BETTER--

COME WITH ME, SON.

WITHIN MINUTES, JUNIOR INVENTS A WILD STORY WHICH HE USES TO DIVERT HIS FATHER'S ATTENTION...

YEAH, DAD! SHE TRIED TO PUT HER HANDS UNDER MY PAJAMAS!

I THOUGHT SHE WAS PECULIAR BUT THIS TEARS IT!

JUNIOR, I DON'T WANT YOU TO GET WITHIN 10 FEET OF THAT GIRL AGAIN!

CORA NOTICES THAT JUNIOR DOES HIS BEST TO KEEP AS MUCH DISTANCE BETWEEN THEM AS POSSIBLE...

CORA, COME SIT DOWN NOW, THE CEREMONY'S ABOUT TO BEGIN!

234

THE BIBLE TELLS US THAT EVE WAS MADE OF ADAM'S RIB SO THAT HE WOULD HAVE A HELPER IN LIFE...

PRETTY BASIC.

NOW, MOST YOUNG PEOPLE MEET, FALL IN LOVE AND SETTLE DOWN -- WITH THE EXCEPTION HERE OF PRIVATE LLOYD'S SISTER WHO HAS DECIDED NOT TO TAKE THIS PATH --

?!?

TOO STUNNED TO MOVE, CORA IS DIMLY AWARE OF THE REST OF THE CEREMONY...

PSST! CORA! STAND UP! EVERYBODY'S WAITING ON YOU!

THEY ALL MOVE INTO AN ADJOINING ROOM FOR THE RECEPTION...

CHOFF!

YOU SANG BEAUTIFULLY.

THANKS! AND DON'T WORRY HONEY. I DIDN'T GET MARRIED UNTIL I WAS 31.

carol Lay

I MET MY HUSBAND THE PREACHER WHEN I WENT ON A BLIND DATE WITH HIM AND HIS BROTHER AND MY TWIN SISTER CARLOTTA. I KNEW I WAS GOING TO MARRY HIM BEFORE THE EVENING WAS OUT.

...OLD MAID...

I KNOW A NICE-LOOKING ARTIST YOU'D PROBABLY LIKE... HE LIVES RIGHT OUTSIDE OF ST. PAUL-- MAKES JEWELRY & BELTS...

CHILD MOLESTER

THERE IS NO BOOZE IN THE PUNCH...

MRS. BREWSER CATCHES CORA ALONE...

I'M GLAD YOU MANAGED TO BEHAVE YOURSELF!

TIME SEEMS TO REALLY DRAG...

BUT THEY FINALLY SAY THEIR GOOD-BYES AND LEAVE, HEADING BACK TO THE BIG CITY TO CATCH AN EVENING FLIGHT TO LOS ANGELES...

THERE'S NO PLACE LIKE HOME... THERE'S NO PLACE LIKE HOME...

BY THE TIME CORA GETS ON THE PLANE SHE'S SAPPED BUT STILL UNABLE TO SLEEP FROM TOO MANY RUMINATIONS...

WHAT HAPPENED? I WAS WEARING MY SQUAREST OUTFIT.

AFTER A FEW HOURS, CORA IS BACK IN HER OWN APARTMENT UNTIL FRIENDS DROP BY AND DRAG HER OFF TO A NIGHT-CLUB WHERE A PERFORMANCE ARTIST IS SLASHING GREEN OOZE OUT OF DILDOED DUMMIES AND SCREAMING THE MOST EXQUISITE GIBBERISH...

THAT'S MORE LIKE IT...

©1983 CAROL LAY

235

gilbert HerNaNdez

The WHISPERING TREE by BETO
APR-84

WHILE OFELIA'S BUSY, DORALIS, I WANNA SHOW YOU SOMETHING SCARY THAT MARTIN EL LOCO TOLD ME ABOUT...

NO..! I DON'T WANNA BE SCARED, GUADALUPE!

IT'S NOT SCARY SCARY! IT'S FUNNY SCARY!

SCARY'S NOT FUNNY!

SEE THAT TREE? WELL, A LONG, LONG TIME AGO A LADY DIED, AND THEY BURIED HER RIGHT THERE... THEN THE TREE GREW ON THAT SAME SPOT!

WAS SHE A PRINCESS?

NO! SHE WAS A BRUJA!

A--A BRU--BRU-- BRU--

BRUJA- BREW'-HAH ⟨WITCH⟩

3

the Goat

I'M SITTING AT THE BAR, RIGHT? SO IN COMES THIS GIRL I HADN'T SEEN SINCE JUNIOR HIGH...

BECKY SNYDER WALKED RIGHT PASS ME AND SAT A COUPLE OF STOOLS DOWN. SHE LOOKED BEAT.

I DIDN'T EXPECT HER TO REMEMBER ME BUT I RECOGNIZED HER FROM THAT BIRTHMARK ON HER CHEEK.

BECKY SNYDER. YEAH, SHE WAS ONE OF THOSE KIDS WHO CRIED IN CLASS A LOT.

SHE WAS ALWAYS IN TROUBLE EVEN IF SHE NEVER REALLY BOTHERED ANYONE.

KIDS CALLED HER "THE GOAT". SHE FLUNKED TWICE, I THINK.

LAST TIME I SAW HER WAS ONE OF THE MANY TIMES I WAS CALLED INTO THE OFFICE FOR DITCHING.

IT LOOKED LIKE THE COPS WERE TAKING HER AWAY. I NEVER KNEW WHAT THAT WAS ALL ABOUT.

SO THERE SHE WAS, JUST TWO STOOLS AWAY. WHAT THE HELL, I THOUGHT. I DECIDED I WAS GONNA BUY HER A DRINK. I DIDN'T NOTICE THAT BIG GIRL COME INTO THE PLACE.

LIGHT BEER

239

THE BIG GIRL QUIETLY WALKS OVER TO SNYDER AND PROCEEDS TO PUMMEL THE HELL OUT OF HER.

THE BIG GIRL LEFT AS QUIETLY AS SHE CAME IN. BECKY JUST SAT THERE ALL BEAT TO HELL, RED AS A BEET, ALL EMBARRASSED AND KIND OF GRINNING...

THE ENTIRE JOINT WAS STILL AS A TOMB.

BECKY GOT UP AND LEFT AFTER A FEW MINUTES. I SAT ALONE ON MY STOOL LISTENING TO THE OTHERS IN THE BAR TRYING TO TOP EACH OTHER WITH THEIR OWN REACTIONS...

...AND I WAS JUST STANDING BACK HERE, AND...

...AND I WAS, AND I WAS...

BETO 99 + XAIME 8

My Prayer

I THINK WE MAY AS WELL CHANGE THE SLOGAN ON OUR CURRENCY FROM "IN GOD WE TRUST" TO "T.G.I.F." (THANK GOD ITS FRIDAY.) I MEAN, WHO ARE WE KIDDING?! **LABOR**, IN THIS CULTURE IS JUST A VACUOUS EXCUSE TO GET TO THE WEEKEND. ITS AN ATTITUDE THAT SUGGESTS THAT WHAT WE'RE DOIN' DURING THE WORK WEEK IS NOT THE REAL THING.

LOOK, HOWEVER AT THE FLIMSY HEM ON THAT "DESIGNER" GARMENT YOU PAID A FORTUNE FOR, OR SPEND HOURS TRYING TO UNRAVEL A CLERICAL ERROR YOU ARE BEING CHARGED FOR, AND IT BECOMES APPARENT.

... I WISH THAT PEOPLE WOULD REALIZE THAT ALTHO WE HAVE TO WORK TO SURVIVE, THE WORLD IS A BETTER PLACE WHEN THE STITCHES ARE SEWN CAREFULLY.

PTBBBB

241

carol tyler

243

FUNSLOWER FEEDS

AN OBSESSION

BEFORE SEX AND DRUGS AND ROCK AND ROLL THERE WERE, COMICS, CANDY, AND... SUNFLOWER SEEDS...

NO! AND GET OUT OF THE ROOM!

...HOURS OF IDLE TIME, RACKING MY CHEEKS AND THE ROOF OF MY MOUTH WITH SALT AND SEED...

THO' NOT EVERYONE CAN APPRECIATE THE NUANCE AND RITUAL OF SUNFLOWER SEEDS,

ENERGETIC STYLE, USING HANDS TO CRACK AND PEEL (GIRL STYLE)

PRO-STYLE, SEVEN OR EIGHT AT A TIME IN THE CHEEK, NO HANDS

THE FAMOUS SHELLS ON THE LIPS WHILE TALKING STYLE, VERY COOL

I CHERISH MEMORIES OF LONG BULL-SESSIONS OVER A 15¢ BAG AMONG BUDS..

...AND CRACKING JOKES IN P.E., ONE OF THE SAFE TIMES TO SHMOOZE WITH THE BAD PACHUCOS WHO WERE ALSO ADDICTED...

"CHUKES" ALWAYS WORE SWEATS, "NO SHOWING OE LEGS"

...NO PRE-SHELLED SEEDS FOR US! THOSE ARE FOR SISSIES...

SATURDAY MORNING CATECHISM WITH AN EX-NAZI, MALE NUN, BROTHER ANTHONY...

DO YOU UNDERSHTANT YOT I AM SAYINK ABOUT CHEEZUS?

... HE'D PUT UP WITH OUR EATING "PARAKEET" SEEDS WHILE PHYSICALLY RAMMING GOD DOWN OUR THROATS...

...NOW AND AGAIN I'LL SHARE A BAG WITH MY KIDS, BUT THE ZEN ASPECTS ELUDE THEM, SO FAR...

DAD! QUACK DESE FO' ME!

DO MINE TOO DAD!

MARIO '89 ©

OH WELL, WE ALL GOTTA START SOMEPLACE...

jayr pulga

WE LIKE TO GO TO THE RIVER AND KEEP OUR HEADS UNDERWATER FOR AS LONG AS WE CAN. WHEN WE START TO FEEL THAT OUR HEADS ARE NO LONGER ON OUR BODIES BUT

THAT THEY HAVE BEEN PULLED OFF BY THE FORCE OF THE CURRENT OUT OF THE WATER. WE PULL THEM OUT SO QUICKLY IT FEELS AS WE SNAP OUR HEADS BACK IF OUR HEADS SHOOT OFF LIKE

ROCKETS TOWARDS THE SUN. THE HEAT OPENS THE PORES ON OUR FACES AND BURIES OUR EYES IN WATER. TEARS STREAM ACROSS OUR CHEEKS LEAVING BEHIND A TRAIL OF SALT WHICH STAINS THE SKIN.

245

THE SMELL OF ONIONS COOKING MAKES ME FORGET EVERYTHING.

TANGERINES SO SMALL AND SWEET THEY FOLLOW ME EVERYWHERE.

THE FISH IS POPPING IN THE PAN.

AT THE MARKET THEY ARE RAW AND SPLIT DOWN THE MIDDLE.

EACH HALF LAYING NEXT TO EACH OTHER.

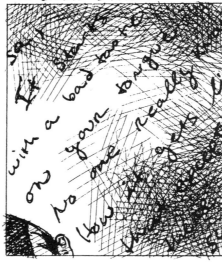

IF YOU LOOK CLOSELY...

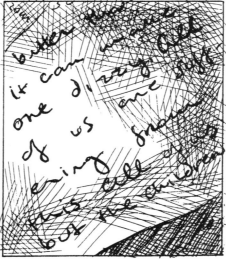

YOU CAN SEE THEIR LUNGS FILL UP WITH AIR...

THEN BLOW IT BACK OUT.

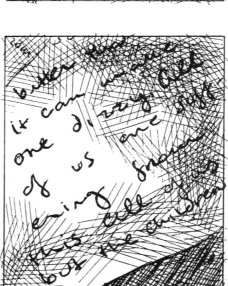

ben katchor

DREAM BOOKS ARE A PERFECTLY LEGAL OUTGROWTH OF THAT ILLEGAL PASTIME OF THE POOR — THE NUMBERS GAME.

LET ME HAVE THE 'BLUE DOLLAR' BOOK

THESE BOOKS PURPORT TO GIVE ADVICE AND A METHOD OF INTERPRETING, IN NUMERICAL TERMS, THE SENSELESS IMAGES WHICH ACCOMPANY SLEEP.

IT IS, SPECIFICALLY, THE LAST THREE DIGITS OF THAT DAY'S HANDLE AT THE RACE TRACK,

WHICH THE READER HOPES TO HAVE HAD CRYPTICALLY ANNOUNCED IN HIS *SLEEP*.

THE NUMBERS GAME, THUS PLAYED, IS NO LONGER A MATTER OF CHANCE, BUT A QUESTION OF ESOTERIC KNOWLEDGE.

I BUY SWEEPINGS

THE NEWSSTANDS, GROCERIES AND CANDY STORES IN POOR NEIGHBORHOODS, OPENLY DISPLAY DOZENS OF THESE BOOKS.

JUST A MINUTE

THEY ALSO SELL NEAR HOSPITALS AND BUS STOPS.

FIFTY CENTS A POUND

HOW CAN HE MAKE A LIVING!

MOST ARE ISSUED ON A DAILY BASIS

THESE BOOKS ARE THE PRODUCT OF AN HONEST, ALBEIT SEMI-MYSTICAL, SMALL INDUSTRY.

©1989 BEN KATCHOR

CONTINUED NEXT WEEK

ben katchor

LAST WEEK—THE MAN WAITING FOR THE BUS, BUYS BARBER SHOP SWEEPINGS FOR A LIVING. HE ALSO READS THE "BLUE DOLLAR" DREAM BOOK BEFORE PLACING HIS BET IN THE NUMBERS GAME.

THE ORACLE OF THE "BLUE DOLLAR" BOOK SPENDS HIS DAY IN A SELF-SERVICE RESTAURANT.

HE IS A FORTY-SEVEN YEAR OLD MAN WITH A BACKGROUND IN THEOLOGY.

HE CLAIMS TO HAVE A SLEEP FREE OF DREAMS

HOWEVER, THE OBJECTS OF HIS DIURNAL VISION ARE, MIRACULOUSLY, EMBLAZONED WITH SIGNIFICANT NUMBERS.

HE RECORDS IT ALL ON NAPKINS AND PAPER PLATES.

WHEN THE RESTAURANT CLOSES, HE GOES TO HIS FURNISHED ROOM, AND IN A FRENZY, PUTS TOGETHER THE NEXT DAY'S ISSUE.

HE KNOWS IN WHICH OLD MAGAZINES AND NEWSPAPERS TO FIND JUST THE RIGHT "ARTWORK" AND "NUMERAL" TO ILLUSTRATE HIS VISIONS.

HE LEAVES A BLANK SPACE ON PAGE TEN FOR THAT DAY'S HANDLE AT THE RACE TRACK.

NO ONE ASKS HIM TO EXPLAIN THOSE PARTICULARLY SLAP-DASH PAGES.

HE DELIVERS THE FINISHED JOB IN PERSON AND IS GIVEN TWO TWENTIES AND A TEN BY THE BARTENDER.

CONTINUED NEXT WEEK

© 1989 BEN KATCHOR

CONTINUED NEXT WEEK

ben katchor

CONTINUED NEXT WEEK

ben katchor

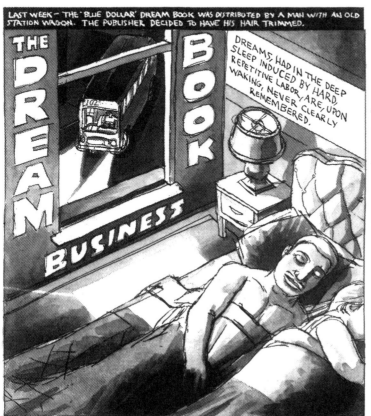

252

eddie campbell

IN THE DAYS OF THE ACE ROCK'N'ROLL CLUB

JAN 79

dapper John minds ⚯ the baby 🍼

WAHHHH

MUST BE FEEDING TIME, JOHN .. YOU CAN USE THE BACK ROOM IF YOU LIKE

SWEEET

7-1

SUCH A SITUATION, OF COURSE, COULDN'T MAR DAPPER JOHN MARVIN'S SPECIAL REPUTATION, THOUGH IT DID TAX HIS RESOURCES. IT SHOULD HAVE BEEN SIMPLE:-

THINK YOU COULD SLEEP AWAY THIS WEEKEND, SON?

SURE, DAD, WHAT'S ON?

I GOT ME SECCETRY COMINK ROUND WHY DON'TCHER POP OVER YOUR SISTER'S. I FINK SHE WANTS TO SEE YOU ABOUT SUMMINK—

DIDN'T KNOW WELDERS 'AD SECRETARIES.

254

7-2

7-4

258

7-6

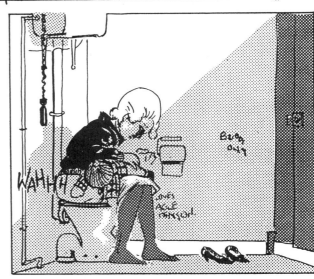

How My Family Encouraged Me to Become an Artist!

©1987 DORI SEDA

AT THE AGE OF TWENTY-EIGHT, I REALIZED I'D BEEN HAD.

I WONDER IF THEY'LL TAKE FOOD STAMPS FOR A REFILL OF COFFEE.

A FELLOW ARTIST AND FELLOW MEMBER OF THE "UNEMPLOYMENT CLUB"

BUT I WAS IRREPARABLY AN ARTIST, AND I WASN'T FIT TO DO ANYTHING ELSE.

WHY CAN'T I GET INTERESTED IN COMPUTERS LIKE NORMAL PEOPLE MY AGE?

IT'S ALWAYS AN ORDEAL WHEN I GO HOME TO VISIT.

DORI, I'M SENDING YOU SOME MONEY FOR CLOTHES-I WANT YOU TO FEEL UH....COMFORTABLE WHEN YOU COME HOME.

POOR DORI, SHE ALWAYS LOOKS LIKE A BUM.

POOR MOM, SHE THINKS I'M A BUM.

MY CARTOONING CAREER DOESN'T SEEM TO IMPRESS MY RELATIVES.

AN' THIS IS "LONELY NIGHTS," MY SOLO BOOK- I DREW THE WHOLE THING!!

EW!

WE DID THIS TO HER.

I THINK SHE'S ON DRUGS.

I OFTEN WONDER ABOUT MY FATHER'S MOTIVATION WHEN HE TAUGHT ME TO DRAW- IT'S KIND OF LIKE THROWING A KID TO THE WOLVES.

HA!

SNARL!

SNORT!

GARR!

I'VE NOTICED THAT MY BROTHER AND MY COUSINS ARE NOT ENCOURAGING THEIR KIDS TO BE ARTISTS.

DON'T DO THAT!! YOU'RE GONNA WIND UP LIKE YOUR WEIRD AUNT DORI!!

The End

THE ADVENTURES OF HERGÉ.

50 YEARS AGO

262

joost swarte

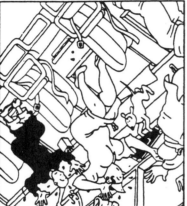

263

AH, THERE HE IS.

THE PRINTER IS WAITING FOR THE PHOTOS, REMY. WE MUST HURRY.

I SAW SOME OF YOUR DRAWINGS AT WALLEZ'S HOUSE... THEY WERE PRETTY GOOD... THEY MADE ME THINK OF ZIG AND PUCE AND BECASSINE... IF YOU WORK..

BOCK

KOEKELBE

A SHORT WHILE LATER.

GOOD. JUST IN TIME.

AH, REMY. DID YOU HAVE A NICE TRIP?

OF COURSE, DIRECTOR. AND WHAT'S MORE, I HAD AN OPPORTUNITY TO EXAMINE THE AIRPLANE CLOSELY! THE CREW EXPLAINED TO ME HOW EVERYTHING WORKED! I COULD FILL UP A WHOLE MAGAZINE!

EVEN AFTER FLYING LOSES ITS NOVELTY, AERIAL TRANSPORT WILL CONTINUE TO BE POPULAR. AND ABOVE ALL, IT CREATES A FEELING OF TOTAL SAFETY AND SECURITY.

I'M GOING TO SEND YOU UP TO SEE THE EDITOR OF "ENGINEERING AND PRODUCTION" MAGAZINE. A BRIGHT AND OBSERVANT YOUNG MAN LIKE YOU WOULD HAVE A BETTER FUTURE THERE THAN DOING CHILDREN'S BOOKS.

TERRIBLE NEWS. AN AIRPLANE HAS CRASHED. A JUNKER FLYING FROM MELBROEK TO COLOGNE. THE THREE PASSENGERS WERE WOUNDED, BUT ALL THREE MEMBERS OF THE CREW ARE DEAD.

BELGIQUE
2JOO§
BELGIE

ISN'T THAT THE SAME AIRPLANE YOU WERE JUST ON?

UH... ER, YES, FATHER.

LISTEN, REMY. YOUR SKETCHES ARE QUITE GOOD. KEEP ON DOING THEM.

Vingtie
Siecl

END

r. crumb

MUCH TO-DO HAS BEEN MADE OVER THE U.S. ARMY GENERAL OF WORLD-WAR II, GEORGE S. PATTON. WELL, THIS STORY ISN'T ABOUT HIM. THIS ONE'S ABOUT CHARLEY PATTON, A HUMBLE MISSISSIPPI DELTA BLUES SINGER WHO DIED IN 1934. THE ONLY THING THIS PATTON HAD IN COMMON WITH THE RENOWNED GENERAL WAS THAT HIS NAME, TOO, WAS...

PATTON

by R.Crumb
1984

CHARLEY PATTON LIVED MOST OF HIS LIFE ON THE VAST DOCKERY PLANTATION IN THE BOTTOMLANDS OF THE MISSISSIPPI DELTA. HE WAS A RAMBLER, A SHIFTLESS NO-GOOD WHO LIVED OFF WOMEN AND PASSED HIS TIME IN TOTAL IDLENESS.
   HE WAS ALSO A GREAT BLUES PERFORMER WHOSE POWERFUL EFFECT ON THE BLUES AND ROCK AND ROLL IS STILL FELT TODAY, THOUGH FEW PEOPLE EVER HEARD OF HIM. THE MUSIC HE PLAYED AND SANG CAN IN NO WAY BE DESCRIBED. IT MUST BE LISTENED TO.

RECOMMENDED LISTENING: "CHARLEY PATTON" YAZOO L-1020, A DOUBLE ALBUM WITH 28 OF HIS RECORDED SONGS

MOST OF THE TIME HE WORKED ALONE, AT PARTIES AND JUKE JOINTS ON THE PLANTATION, OR IN NEAR-BY TOWNS. HE WAS A POPULAR ENTERTAINER WITH THE FIELD-HANDS, WITH HIS DYNAMIC, DRIVING DANCE RHYTHMS, HIS THEATRICS, CLOWNING AND STUNTS LIKE PLAYING THE GUITAR BE-HIND HIS BACK. WHEN THE GOOD TIMES WERE READY TO ROLL BACK IN "THE QUARTER" CHARLEY WAS THE MAN THEY WANTED!

FOR THE POOR, ISOLATED BLACK PEOPLE WHO LIVED AND WORKED ON THESE PLANTATIONS, IT WAS A WAY OF LIFE LITTLE DIFFERENT FROM THE DAYS OF SLAVERY.

BUT EVERY FARM AND EVERY TOWN HAD ITS MUSICIANS. THERE WERE SONGSTERS AND GUITAR PLAYERS, FIDDLERS AND BANJO PICKERS.

THE BLUES WAS A NEW STYLE OF PLAYING WHEN CHARLEY, AS A TEEN-AGER, FIRST LEARNED IT FROM AN OLDER MUSICIAN AT DOCKERY'S IN THE EARLY 1900s. HIS NAME WAS HENRY SLOAN.

HENRY SLOAN MAY WELL HAVE BEEN THE EARLY BLUESMAN THAT W.C. HANDY HEARD WHILE WAITING FOR A TRAIN IN TUTWILER, MISSISSIPPI IN 1903.

THE NEW COMMERCIALIZED BLUES WERE SUNG IN THEATRES AND CABARETS BY REFINED BLACK WOMEN ENTERTAINERS, BACKED BY THE JAZZ BANDS THEN EMERGING ON THE SHOW BIZ SCENE.

HANDY WAS A SUCCESSFUL SCHOOLED MUSICIAN WHO WAS SO INSPIRED BY THE MUSIC OF THE UNKNOWN BLUES SINGER THAT HE WENT ON TO WRITE "THE ST. LOUIS BLUES," "YELLOW DOG BLUES," "MEMPHIS BLUES" AND MANY OTHER POPULAR TUNES USING THE BLUES FORM.

I HATE TO SEE-E-E... THAT EVENING SUN GO DOWN...

THIS TIN-PAN ALLEY BLUES BARELY TOUCHED THE REMOTE RURAL BLACK PEOPLE OF THE DELTA REGION, WHERE THE REAL DOWN-TO-EARTH BLUES CONTINUED TO EVOLVE AS AN INTENSE AND ELO-QUENT EXPRESSION OF THEIR LIVES. AND THEY ALL CAME TO LEARN FROM CHARLEY PATTON. HE WAS RECOGNIZED AS THE HOT-TEST BLUES PLAYER BY OTHER MUSICIANS AS WELL AS BY THE CROWDS HE PLAYED FOR.

TOMMY JOHNSON, SON HOUSE, HOWLIN' WOLF, AND OTHER GREAT BLUES SINGERS CAME TO LISTEN AND LEARN FROM PATTON. SOME OF THEM WENT ON TO BECOME LEGENDS IN THEIR OWN RIGHT.

EDDIE "SON" HOUSE   HOWLIN' WOLF   TOMMY JOHNSON   BUKKA WHITE

FORTUNATELY FOR US, PATTON AND SOME OF THE OTHERS WERE APPROACHED BY COMMERCIAL RECORD COMPANY SCOUTS IN THE LATE '20s TO MAKE RECORDS.

SAY, I HEAR YOU PLAY A PRETTY MEAN GUITAR...

THE MUSICIANS WERE PAID TO TRAVEL TO NORTHERN CITIES TO RECORD, OR BROUGHT TO TEMPORARY STUDIOS SET UP IN LOCAL HOTELS.

HERE, HAVE A LITTLE SOMETHIN'

THANK Y' SUH...

THE RECORD COMPANIES RECORDED THESE REGIONAL BLUES SINGERS IN THE HOPES OF SELLING PHONOGRAPH MACHINES TO BLACK PEOPLE.

AND WITH THE PURCHASE OF THIS FINE PHONOGRAPH YOU RE-CIEVE, FREE OF CHARGE, THREE OF THE LATEST BLUES HITS!!

WITH THE ONCOMING GREAT DEPRESSION, POOR PEOPLE STOPPED BUYING RECORD PLAYERS ALTOGETHER. WHAT WAS LEFT OF THE RECORDING INDUSTRY LOST INTEREST IN RURAL MUSICIANS AND STAYED WITH THE MORE PROFESSIONAL URBAN BLUESMEN LIKE WASHBOARD SAM, TAMPA RED AND BIG BILL BROONZY.

BUT THE EXTENSIVE RECORDING OF COUNTRY BLUES IN THE TWENTIES HAS LEFT US WITH A RICH CULTURAL HERITAGE. FORTUNATELY, MOST OF THE RARE OLD 78s HAVE BEEN REISSUED BY COLLECTORS ON SMALL LABELS, SO THAT WE CAN STILL ENJOY THIS GREAT MUSIC TODAY.

ALMOST ALL THE ENTHUSIASM FOR PATTON'S MUSIC NOW COMES FROM WHITE, UPPER-MIDDLE CLASS AFICIONADOES AND A FEW ROCK MUSICIANS. ALL THE RESEARCH ON HIS LIFE HAS BEEN DONE BY WHITE ACADEMICS. IT SEEMS THE OLD BLUES IS STILL TOO VIVID A REMINDER TO BLACK PEOPLE OF AN OPPRESSIVE, "UNCLE TOM" PAST THEY'D RATHER FORGET ABOUT.

IF HE WERE STILL ALIVE, CHARLEY WOULD SURELY CONSIDER ALL THIS FUSS BITTERLY IRONIC. IN HIS TIME NO WHITE PEOPLE LISTENED TO THE RAW KIND OF BLUES HE PLAYED. IN FACT, CHARLEY HAD VERY LITTLE CONTACT WITH WHITES AT ALL.

MRS. KEITH DOCKERY IN AN INTERVIEW, 1979

EVEN RESPECTABLE, CHURCH-GOING BLACKS CONSIDERED HIM AND HIS KIND AS "BAD NIGGERS" AND THE BLUES WAS LOOKED UPON AS THE "DEVIL'S MUSIC."

PATTON'S FATHER WAS A HARD-WORKING FARMER AND A DEVOUT CHRISTIAN. HE WAS NOT PLEASED WHEN HE FOUND OUT THAT HIS YOUNG SON WAS PLAYING THAT SINFUL MUSIC.

268

WHEN STERN WARNINGS FAILED, CHARLEY WAS TAKEN TO THE WOODSHED FOR A HARSHER TASTE OF CHRISTIAN JUSTICE.

I TOLE YOU TO KEEP AWAY FROM THEM LOW-LIFE PEOPLES!

LATER HIS FATHER'S HEART SOFTENED TOWARD THE WAYWARD SON, AND HE BOUGHT CHARLEY A GUITAR.

IN THESE EARLY DAYS HE WAS PLAYING AROUND THE NEIGHBORHOOD WITH THE CHATMON FAMILY, A STRINGBAND GROUP THAT PLAYED RAGTIME, MINSTREL AND TIN-PAN ALLEY TUNES AT SOCIAL AFFAIRS, PICNICS AND PARTIES.

BUT EVEN THIS MUSIC WAS TOO TAME FOR THE INTENSE, SEETHING YOUNG PATTON. HE WAS IRRESISTABLY DRAWN TO THE MORE PASSIONATE AND LESS WHITE MUSIC OF HENRY SLOAN, WITH IT'S MORE COMPLEX RHYTHMS.

HEY, BOY, YOU WANNA PLAY SOME TUNES? COME ON IN THE HOUSE!

CHARLEY WAS UNDER THE SPELL OF THE BLUES AND FOLLOWED HENRY SLOAN AROUND FOR YEARS, TRYING TO GRASP THE RUDIMENTS OF THIS NEW MUSICAL APPROACH.

HIS FAMILY NEVER SAW HIM MUCH ANY MORE. HE WANDERED ABOUT, PICKING UP THE WAYS OF MIDNIGHT RAMBLERS, DRINKING HEAVILY, AND LIVING OFF WOMEN WHO COOKED IN WHITE PEOPLE'S KITCHENS.

SHE BRING ME TH'MEAT SHE BRING ME LARD...

WHEN THINGS WENT BAD HE WOULD REPENT AND TAKE UP THE BIBLE, AND RESOLVE HENCEFORTH TO PUT HIS LIFE IN THE SERVICE OF THE LORD BY PREACHING THE GOSPEL.

THESE CONVERSIONS NEVER LASTED LONG. CHARLEY COULDN'T STAY AWAY FROM THE LOOSE WOMEN, THE GOOD TIMES, AND THE MOONSHINE LIQUOR.

PATTON WAS KNOWN FOR BEING "HIGH-TEMPERED," "FLIGHTY," AND FOR HAVING A "BIG MOUTH" WHICH OFTEN GOT HIM INTO FIGHTS, THOUGH HE WAS ILL-EQUIPPED TO DEFEND HIMSELF PHYSICALLY.

IT IS ALSO WELL-KNOWN THAT HE FOUGHT VIOLENTLY WITH HIS WOMEN. "IF THOSE WOMEN MADE HIM MAD, HE'D JUS' FIGHT, AND, YOU KNOW, KNOCK 'EM OUT WITH THAT OLD GUITAR," CLAIMED AN OLD ACQUAINTANCE.

SOMETIME AROUND 1931 SOMEONE TRIED TO CUT HIS THROAT, BUT PATTON SURVIVED WITH AN UGLY SCAR.

"I KNEW ONE OF HIS WIVES, NAMED LIZZIE, AND SHE SAID ONE DAY HE JUST WALKED OFF WITH HIS GUITAR AND NEVER CAME BACK. SHE HADN'T DONE NOTHIN' TO HIM. HE HADN'T DONE NOTHIN' TO HER."

"WELL, AFTER THAT SHE WOULD TALK A LOT ABOUT HOW MEAN HE WAS. BUT SHE KEPT HIS PICTURE RIGHT THERE ON HER MANTEL. SHE KEPT IT 'TIL THE DAY SHE DIED."

MOST OF THE BLUES RECORDED AT HIS FIRST SESSIONS IN 1929 WERE CELEBRATIONS OF THE WILD TIMES, BOASTS OF HIS SEXUAL ADVENTURES, JEALOUS WOMEN, TWO-TIMING WOMEN, DRINKING AND CAROUSING. IN "IT WONT BE LONG" PATTON SINGS, "GOT A LONG TALL WOMAN, TALL LIKE A CHERRY TREE, SHE GETS UP 'FORE DAY AND SHE PUT THE THING ON ME."

IN "TOM RUSHEN BLUES" HE SINGS ABOUT GETTING DRUNK AND THROWN IN JAIL. "I LAY DOWN LAST NIGHT, HOPIN' I WOULD HAVE MY PEACE, BUT WHEN I WOKE UP, TOM RUSHEN WAS SHAKIN' ME. WHEN YOU GET IN TROUBLE, NO USE TO SCREAMIN' AN' CRYIN', TOM RUSHEN WILL TAKE YOU BACK TO PRISON HOUSE FLYIN'."

ONE OF PATTON'S MOST POPULAR RECORDS, "HIGH WATER EVERYWHERE" WAS A WAILING LAMENT ABOUT THE MISSISSIPPI RIVER FLOOD OF 1927. THE GREAT RIVER OVERFLOWED THE LEVEES AND WASHED OVER THE LAND. "BACKWATER DONE ROSE AT SUMNER, DROVE POOR CHARLEY DOWN THE LINE. LORD, I TELL THE WORLD THE WATER DONE JUMPED THROUGH THIS TOWN."

"IT WAS FIFTY MEN AND CHILDREN COME TO SINK AND DROWN, OH LORDIE, WOMEN AND GROWN MEN DOWN, OH WOMEN AND CHILDREN SINKIN' DOWN."

"I COULDN'T SEE NOBODY HOME AND WASN'T NO ONE TO BE FOUND."

SEVERAL OF HIS SONGS WERE ABOUT MOVING ON, LEAVING A WOMAN, WANDERING... "I'M GOIN' AWAY, SWEET MAMA, DON'T YOU WANT TO GO? TAKE GOD TO TELL WHEN I'LL BE BACK HERE ANYMORE." (SCREAMIN' AND HOLLERIN' THE BLUES)
"SOME THESE DAY, YOU GONNA MISS YOUR HONEY, I KNOW YOU'RE GONNA MISS ME, SWEET DREAMS, FOR I BE GOIN' AWAY." (SOME THESE DAYS I'LL BE GONE)

MOSTLY HE SANG ABOUT HAVING A GOOD TIME; "I LIKE TO FUSS AND FIGHT, I LIKE TO FUSS AND FIGHT, LORD, AND GET SLOPPY DRUNK OFF A BOTTLE AND BALL AND WALK THE STREETS ALL NIGHT." (ELDER GREEN BLUES)

BUT THE WORDS WERE NOT THE MAIN POINT OF PATTON'S MUSIC. THEY ARE BARELY UNDERSTANDABLE MOST OF THE TIME AND IMPOSSIBLE SOMETIMES. EVEN SON HOUSE HAS SAID THAT CHARLEY'S WORDS WERE DIFFICULT TO MAKE OUT. CHARLEY WAS PLAYING DANCE MUSIC MOSTLY, FOR SATURDAY NIGHT PARTIES WHERE THERE WAS A LOT OF NOISE AND CARRYING ON, AND POTENT CORN LIQUOR FLOWED FREELY.

272

HIS VOICE WAS USED AS A MUSICAL INSTRUMENT. HE SHOUTED, SCREAMED, BELLOWED AND GROWLED. HE BEAT ON HIS GUITAR, POUNDING OUT HEAVY RHYTHMS FOR LONG STRETCHES, SOMETIMES HALF AN HOUR, WHILE THE CROWD DANCED.

HAYS McMULLEN, A CONTEMPORARY OF PATTON'S, REMEMBERS: "I'VE SEEN CHARLEY PATTON JUST BUMP ON HIS GUITAR 'STEAD OF PICKIN' IT... I BUMPED ON IT TOO. COLORED FOLKS GET DANCIN' GONNA DANCE ALL NIGHT AND I'D GET TIRED, SO I'D GET 'EM GOOD 'N' STARTED, YOU KNOW, I'D BE HOLLERIN', AND THEN I'D JUST BE KNOCKIN' ON THE BOX WHEN THE MUSIC GET GOING."

PATTON'S BEST FRIEND SEEMS TO HAVE BEEN WILLIE BROWN. AFTER YEARS OF HANGING OUT WITH CHARLEY AND STUDYING HIS WAY OF SINGING AND PLAYING, WILLIE BROWN BECAME A TOP-NOTCH DELTA BLUES MUSICIAN HIMSELF.

THEY SOMETIMES PLAYED TOGETHER FOR DANCES, WILLIE FILLING IN THE RHYTHM WHILE CHARLIE THREW HIS GUITAR UP IN THE AIR, CAUGHT IT BETWEEN HIS LEGS, AND RAN THROUGH HIS OTHER TRICKS TO AMUSE THE CROWD.

TOMMY JOHNSON, FROM SOUTHERN MISSISSIPPI, ALSO CAME TO LEARN FROM THESE TWO GREAT BLUES MASTERS. BACK HOME, HE TOLD HIS BROTHER LEDELL THAT HE HAD LEARNED THE BLUES BY SELLING HIS SOUL TO THE DEVIL.

"I ASKED HIM HOW," LEDELL LATER RECOUNTED. "HE SAID, IF YOU WANT TO LEARN HOW TO PLAY ANYTHING AND LEARN HOW TO MAKE SONGS YOURSELF, YOU TAKE YOUR GUITAR AND YOU GO TO WHERE A ROAD CROSSES THAT WAY, WHERE A CROSSROAD IS. BE SURE TO GET THERE JUST A LITTLE 'FORE TWELVE O'CLOCK THAT NIGHT...YOU HAVE YOUR GUITAR AND BE PLAYING A PIECE SITTING THERE BY YOURSELF."

"A BIG BLACK MAN WILL WALK UP THERE AND TAKE YOUR GUITAR, AND HE'LL TUNE IT AND THEN HE'LL PLAY A PIECE AND HAND IT BACK TO YOU. THAT'S THE WAY I LEARNED HOW TO PLAY ANYTHING I WANT."

ANOTHER GREAT DELTA SINGER WHO CAME TO KNOW CHARLEY PATTON WAS SON HOUSE. HOUSE HAD JUST GOTTEN OUT OF PARCHMAN, A MISSISSIPPI PENAL FARM, AFTER A TWO-YEAR TERM FOR SHOOTING AND KILLING A MAN IN A FIGHT IN 1928. PATTON LIKED SON HOUSE'S MUSIC AND INVITED HIM TO COME ALONG TO A RECORDING SESSION IN GRAFTON, WISCONSIN, WITH HIMSELF AND WILLIE BROWN.

ALSO GOING ALONG WAS LOUISE JOHNSON, A YOUNG GIRL WHO PLAYED A POWERFUL BOOGIE WOOGIE PIANO BLUES IN A LOCAL JUKE JOINT. PATTON WAS IMPRESSED WITH HER PLAYING AS WELL AS HER LOOKS AND HAD BEGUN COURTING HER.

HOUSE BRAGGED YEARS LATER HOW HE'D STOLEN THE GIRL PIANO PLAYER AWAY FROM CHARLEY ON THE TRIP UP TO GRAFTON; "CHARLEY, HE'S MAD. HE'S SITTING IN THE FRONT. RIGHT ALONG I COMMENCE TO LEANING OVER TALKING TRASH TO HER. I SAY, 'I REALLY KINDA LIKE YOU, GAL,' AND WE TAKE ANOTHER BIG SWALLOW."

"SO THEY HAVE A LITTLE HOTEL THERE IN GRAFTON WHERE THE RECORDERS STAY AT....SO I COME UP, AND THEY'S TELLING ME 'BOUT THE MAN DONE BEEN HERE AND GIVE US ALL THE KEYS. I SAID, 'WHERE DID HE GO, 'CAUSE HE AIN' GIVE ME NO KEY,' AND SO LOUISE SAY, 'YES HE DID.' I SAY, 'NO HE DIDN'T. SAY, 'I GOT ME AND YOUR KEY.' I SAY, 'OH, OH, THAT'S IT THEN'...AND THAT'S THE WAY IT HAPPENED...ME AND HER STAYED IN OUR LITTLE ROOM."

BY THE MID 'TWENTIES A YOUNGER CROP OF BLUES PLAYERS WERE COMING UP STRONG IN THE DELTA. AMONG THESE WAS A HIGH-STRUNG TEEN-AGER NAMED ROBERT JOHNSON. HE LIVED NEAR WILLIE BROWN AND STARTED COMING AROUND TO PICK UP THE BLUES FROM BROWN, PATTON, AND SON HOUSE.

THE OLDER MUSICIANS DISDAINED YOUNG JOHNSON'S FALTERING EFFORTS ON THE GUITAR. WHEN THEY WERE DRUNK AND FEELING MEAN, PATTON, BROWN AND HOUSE WOULD OFTEN RIDICULE HIS PLAYING, FINALLY FORCING HIM TO RUN AWAY FROM THE AREA.

A YEAR OR SO LATER, ROBERT JOHNSON RETURNED AND DAZZLED THEM ALL WITH A NEW BLUES GUITAR STYLE USING A DRIVING, HEAVY BASS BEAT THAT HE HAD CREATED ON HIS OWN. IN 1936 AND '37 JOHNSON WOULD RECORD SOME OF THE GREATEST COUNTRY BLUES OF ALL TIME.

PATTON'S HEALTH WAS SERIOUSLY FAILING BY 1930. A HARD, FAST LIFE OF DRINKING CORN LIQUOR AND CHAIN-SMOKING WAS BEGINNING TO TELL ON HIM. HE WAS PROBABLY ONLY IN HIS MID-FORTIES BY THIS TIME.

HIS SONGS BEGAN TAKING ON A MORE OMINOUS, DESPERATE NOTE. IN "BIRD NEST BOUND" HE SEEMED TO YEARN FOR SECURITY AND STABILITY. "IF I WAS A BIRD, MAMA, I WOULD FIND A NEST IN THE HEART OF TOWN, SO WHEN THE TOWN GET LONESOME, I'D BE BIRDNEST BOUND."

"OH I REMEMBER ONE MORNIN', STANDIN' IN MY BABY'S DOOR... BOY, YOU KNOW WHAT SHE TOLD ME? LOOKA HERE, PAPA CHARLEY, I DON'T WANT YOU NO MORE."

BUT THEY STAYED TOGETHER, AND SANG TOGETHER AT PATTON'S LAST RECORDING SESSION IN 1934. IN JANUARY OF THAT YEAR W. R. CALAWAY OF THE AMERICAN RECORD CORPORATION BEGAN LOOKING FOR PATTON TO CUT SOME NEW RECORDS. THE INDUSTRY WAS BEGINNING TO REVIVE SOMEWHAT FROM THE DEPRESSION.

HE FINALLY LOCATED CHARLEY AND BERTHA LEE IN THE LITTLE TOWN OF BELZONI, MISSISSIPPI. THEY WERE BOTH IN JAIL, HAVING BEEN INVOLVED IN A DRUNKEN FRACAS AT A HOUSE PARTY. CALAWAY BAILED THEM OUT.

FROM 1930 ON PATTON LIVED WITH A WOMAN NAMED BERTHA LEE, WHO COOKED FOR WHITE FAMILIES IN THE NEIGHBORHOOD. THE COUPLE MOVED AROUND, HAD VIOLENT ARGUMENTS. PATTON BLAMED HIS FAILING HEALTH ON HER. HE ACCUSED HER OF STARVING HIM. THEY'D GET DRUNK AND GO AT EACH OTHER IN VIOLENT FITS OF RAGE.

HE TOOK THEM WITH HIM BACK TO NEW YORK CITY. PATTON WAS IN VERY BAD SHAPE. HE WAS WEAK, SHORT OF BREATH, AND HAD LOST MUCH OF HIS PERFORMING POWER.

HIS LAST RECORDINGS REVEAL HIS AWARENESS THAT HIS LIFE MAY BE CUT SHORT. IN "POOR ME," HE SINGS, "DON'T THE MOON LOOK PRETTY, SHININ' DOWN THROUGH THE TREE. I CAN SEE BERTHA LEE, LORD, BUT SHE CAN'T SEE ME."

HE AND BERTHA LEE SANG TOGETHER ON THE SONG "OH DEATH." ON THIS RECORD YOU CAN VIVIDLY HEAR THE NEARNESS OF DEATH AND CHARLEY'S HORROR IN THE FACE OF IT.

SEVERAL WEEKS AFTER THIS PATTON LAY ON HIS DEATH BED. FOR A WEEK HE LAID THERE PREACHING, REPEATING OVER AND OVER HIS FAVORITE SERMON, RECORDED BY HIM IN 1929 UNDER THE PSEUDONYM ELDER J.J. HADLEY; "WHEN HE COME DOWN HIS HAIR GONNA BE LIKE LAMB'S WOOL AND HIS EYES LIKE FLAMES OF FIRE, AND EVERY MAN GONNA KNOW HE'S THE SON OF THE TRUE LIVING GOD...'ROUND HIS SHOULDERS GOIN' TO BE A RAINBOW AND HIS FEET LIKE FINE BRASS... AND HE'S GONNA HAVE A TREE BEFORE THE TWELVE MANNERS OF FOOD, AND THE LEAVES GONNA BE HEALING DAMNATION, AND THE BIG ROCK THAT YOU CAN SIT BEHIND, THE WIND CAN'T BLOW AT YOU NO MORE, AND YOU GONNA COUNT THE FOUR-AND-TWENTY ELDERS THAT YOU CAN SIT DOWN AND TALK WITH, AND THAT YOU CAN TALK ABOUT YOUR TROUBLE THAT YOU COME — WORLD YOU JUST COME FROM."

CHARLEY PATTON DIED ON APRIL 28TH, 1934. HIS DEATH WENT UNREPORTED IN THE LOCAL AND NATIONAL PRESS.

A LARGE PORTION OF THE INFORMATION FOR THIS STORY CAME FROM ROBERT PALMER'S FINE BOOK, "DEEP BLUES," PUBLISHED IN 1981 BY VIKING PRESS.

276

picture **YOU** in a **PADDED** bra

empty wig stands
body sculpture
push-up bras
quickie fucks in rusty cars

You're pushed up to here

Sea shell embroidery over sheer

Increases your bust one full size.

Lightly padded

Padded push-up shelf

Wired Undercup

Leno Elastic

278

dynel falls
living dolls
shopping malls
valiums crammed in crystal jars

WANNA START SOMETHING HONEY?

HYPOTHETICAL Quandary

© 1984 BY
HARVEY PEKAR

STORY BY HARVEY PEKAR
ART BY R. CRUMB

SUNDAY MORNING

HMMM... THAT WOMAN FROM THAT BIG PUBLISHER NEVER GOT BACK T'ME. GUESS SHE WASN'T SERIOUS; PROB'LY WANTED A FREE BOOK OR WAS TOO LAZY T'LOOK FOR MY STUFF ON THE STANDS OR SUMP'N'.

279

BUT WHAT IF SHE'D BEEN SERIOUS? WHAT IF THEY'D HAVE PUBLISHED MY STUFF AND IT'D SOLD WELL AND I'D HAVE MADE ENOUGH TO SUPPORT MYSELF AS A WRITER?

HOW IMPORTANT IS THAT TO ME?

IT'D BE NICE NOT TO HAVE TO GET UP EV'RY MORNING AND GO TO WORK, TO BE ABLE TO READ OR WORK ON STORIES AND ARTICLES WHENEVER I FELT LIKE IT.

BUT THEN I'D SORT OF BE OUT OF THE STRUGGLE, SORT OF IN AN IVORY TOWER WATCHING THE MAINSTREAM OF LIFE GO BY RATHER THAN PARTICIPATING IN IT...

I'D BE ALIENATED BUT I WOULDN'T THINK I HAD THE RIGHT TO FEEL BAD ABOUT IT. I MEAN, I'D BE A WELL-PAID, FAMOUS AUTHOR. WHAT RIGHT WOULD I HAVE TO COMPLAIN ABOUT ANYTHING?

MAYBE MY WRITING WOULD SUFFER. I'VE GOT A PRETTY UNIQUE VIEWPOINT NOW...I'M A WRITER BUT IN A LOTTA WAYS I'VE GOT A WORKING MAN'S OUTLOOK ON LIFE. I'D HAVE TO AS LONG AS I'VE WORKED AT REGULAR DAY JOBS.

A COUPLA THOSE, ANNA RYE BREAD...

280

STILL, MAYBE I'M MAKING TOO MUCH OF THIS. AS LONG AS I'M ALIVE I'LL BE FINDING INTERESTING THINGS TO WRITE ABOUT, MEETING INTERESTING PEOPLE...

IF I LIVED A DIFFERENT LIFE I COULD STILL WRITE ABOUT IT.

281

Notes on New Comics Artists

PETER BAGGE (Seattle). Author of **The Bradleys** (Fantagraphics: 1989), and the ongoing comic book serial, **Hate**. "In My Room" copyright © Peter Bagge, 1991. Reprinted by permission of the author.

LYNDA BARRY (Chicago). Author of **Come Over, Come Over** (Harper Perennial: 1990), and other titles. "Jimmy Rodgers" copyright © Lynda Barry, 1991. Reprinted by permission of the author.

MARK BEYER (New York City). Author of **Agony** (Pantheon: 1987), and the syndicated comic strip, **Amy & Jordan**. "The Unpleasant Subway" copyright © Mark Beyer, 1991. Reprinted by permission of the author.

PAQUITO BOLINO (Paris). Work has appeared in **Chemical Imbalance**, and numerous other international underground comics magazines. "The New World" copyright © Pasquito Bolino, 1991. Reprinted by permission of the author.

CHARLES BURNS (Philadelphia). Author of **Hard Boiled Defective Stories** (Pantheon: 1988) & other titles. "Two Covers" copyright © Charles Burns, 1991. Reprinted by permission of the author.

EDDIE CAMPBELL (Brisbane, Australia). Author of **The Complete Alec** (Eclipse: 1990) & numerous other titles. "Dapper John Minds the Baby" copyright © Eddie Campbell, 1991. Reprinted by permission of the author.

MARC CARO (Paris). Author of **Tot** (Le Dernier Terrain Vaque: 1988). "Ticket, Please" copyright © Marc Caro, 1991. Reprinted by permission of the author.

DANIEL CLOWES (Chicago). Author on the ongoing comic book serial, **Eightball** (Fantagraphics Comics). "The Laffin' Spittin' Man copyright © Daniel Clowes, 1991. Reprinted by permission of the author.

ROBERT CRUMB (France). **The Collected Robert Crumb** is currently being published by Fantagraphics Books. "Patton" copyright © R. Crumb, 1991. Reprinted by permission of the author.

HOWARD CRUSE (New York City). Author of **Dancin Nekkid with the Angels** (St. Martin's Press)."Raising Nancies" copyright © Howard Cruse, 1991. Reprinted by permission of the author.

LLOYD DANGLE (San Francisco). Author of **Dangle** (Cats-Head Comics: 1991). "We all Live in a Garbage Barge" copyright © Lloyd Dangle, 1991. Reprinted by permission of the author.

KIM DEITCH (White Plains, New York). Author of **Hollywoodland** (Fantagraphics Books) & many other titles. "The Adventures of Don Carlos Balmori" (Famous Frauds #1) copyright © Kim Deitch, 1991. Reprinted by permission of author.

JULIE DOUCET (Montreal). Author of the ongoing comic book, **Dirty Plotte** (Drawn & Quarterly). "The Robbery" copyright © by Julie Doucet, 1991. Reprinted by permission of the author.

MICHAEL DOUGAN (Seattle). Author of **East Texas, Tales From Behind the Pine Curtain** (Real Comet Press: 1988). "Dennis the Sullen Menace" copyright © Michael Dougan & Dennis Eichhorn, 1991. Reprinted by permission of the authors.

PASCAL DOURY (Paris). Author of **Theo Tete De Mort** (Les Humanoides Associes: 1983) and other titles. "Wonderland" copyright © Pascal Doury, 1991. Reprinted by permission of the author.

DENNIS EICHHORN (Seattle). Author of the ongoing comic book, **Real Stuff**, (Fantagraphics). "Dennis the Sullen Menace" copyright © Dennis Eichhorn and Michael Dougan, 1991. Reprinted by permissions of the authors.

WILL EISNER (Tamarac, Florida). Creator of **The Spirit**, and author of dozens of books. "Summertime" copyright © Will Eisner, 1991. Reprinted by permission of the author.

HUNT EMERSON (London). Author of **Rapid Reflexes** (Knockabout: 1990) & other titles. "Buster in Mouth City copyright © Hunt Emerson, 1991. Reprinted by permission of the author.

MARY FLEENER (Los Angeles). Author of **Hoodoo** (3-D Zone: 1988), and the ongoing comic book, **Slutberger** (Rip Off Press). "Parfume de la Mort" copyright © Mary Fleener, 1991. Reprinted by permission of the author.

DREW FREIDMAN (New York City). Author of **Warts and All** (Penguin: 1990) & other titles. "Laugh Makers" copyright © Drew Freidman, 1991. Reprinted by permission of the author.

RICK GEARY (New York City). Author of **At Home with Rich Geary** (Fantagraphics Books: 1985) and other titles. "Farewell to Charlie Chaplin" copyright © Rick Geary, 1991. Reprinted by permission of the author.

JUSTIN GREEN (Sacramento, California). Author of the immortal **Binky Brown Meets the Blessed Virgin Mary** (Rip Off Press: 1974). "The Taboo Gown" copyright © Justin Green, 1991.

BILL GRIFFITH (San Francisco). Creator of **Zippy, The Pinhead** comic strip, syndicated in over 75 papers nationally by King Features. "Dollyboy" copyright © Bill Griffith, 1991. Reprinted by permission of the author.

MATT GROENING (Santa Monica). Creator of **Life in Hell**, and **The Simpsons.** "Can We Go To a Gay Bar Tonight" from **The Big Book of Hell** © 1990 by Matt Groening. All Rights Reserved. Reprinted by permission of Pantheon Books, a division of Random House, NY.

CLIFF HARPER (London). Author of **Anarchy: A Graphic Guide** (Camden Press: 1987). & other titles."The Black Freighter" copyright © Cliff Harper, 1991. Reprinted by permission of the author.

RORY HAYES (1950-1979). Author of **Bogeyman Comics** (San Francisco Comic Book Company: 1974). "Terror from the Grave" copyright © San Francisco Comic Book Company. Reprinted by permission of the publisher.

GILBERT HERNANDEZ (Woodland Hills, California). Author of **Blood of Palomar,** co-creator of the ongoing comic book magazine, **Love & Rockets** (Fantagraphics). "The Whispering Tree" copyright © Gilbert Hernandez, 1991. Reprinted by permission of the author.

JAIME HERNANDEZ (Oxnard, California). Author of **The Death of Speedy**, co-creator of the ongoing comic book, **Love & Rockets** (Fantagraphics). "The Goat" copyright © Jaime Hernandez, 1991. Reprinted by permission of the author.

MARIO HERNANDEZ (San Francisco). Regular contributor to **Heck, Buzzard, Rip Off,** and numerous Bay Area underground comic magazines. Co-creator of the ongoing comic book serial, **Love and Rockets**. "Funflower Feeds" copyright © Mario Hernandez, 1991. Reprinted by permission of the author.

BRUCE HILVITZ (Oakland). Editor of **(Kar-ton): New Comics Art Journal**, co-editor, with Lloyd Dangle of **Heck**. "My Ancestors" copyright © Bruce Hilvitz, 1991. Reprinted by permission of the author.

BEN KATCHOR (New York City). Author of the forthcoming book, **Cheap Novelties** (Penguin Books: 1991). "The Dream Book Business" copyright © Ben Katchor, 1991. Reprinted by permission of the author.

KAZ, Kazimieras G. Prapuolenis (Hoboken, New Jersey). Author of **Buzzbombs** (Fantagraphic Books:1987). "Zombies on Broadway" copyright © Kaz, 1991. Reprinted by permission of the author.

ALINE KOMINSKY-CRUMB (France). Author of **Love That Bunch** (Fantagraphics Books: 1981). "Growing Up as Arnie's Girl" copyright © Aline Kominsky-Crumb, 1991. Reprinted by permission of the author.

PETER KUPER (New York City). Author of **New York, New York** (Fantagraphics Books: 1988). "Mr. Cruise" copyright © Peter Kuper, 1991. Reprinted by permission of the author.

KRYSTINE KRYTTRE (San Francisco). Author of **Death Warmed Over** (Cat-Head Comics: 1990). "Dust to Dust" copyright © Krystine Kryttre, 1991. Reprinted by permission of the author.

CAROL LAY (Los Angeles). Author of the ongoing comic book, **Good Girls** (Fantagraphics Books). "Midwestern Wedding" copyright © Carol Lay, 1991. Reprinted by permission of the author.

JACQUES LOUSTAL (Paris). Author of **New York/Miami** (Catalan Communications: 1989) & other titles. "View of the Ocean" copyright © Loustal, 1991. Reprinted by permission of the author.

JAVIER MARISCAL (Barcelona). Author of **Mariscal** (Paris: Le Dernier Terrain Vague, 1983) & other titles. "The Unexpected Journey" copyright © Mariscal, 1991. Reprinted by permission of the author.

LEE MARRS (Berkeley). Author of **Pudge, Girl Blimp** (Star Reach Productions: 1978). "Moonshine Mama" copyright © Lee Marrs, 1991. Reprinted by permission of the author.

MARTI, Marti Riera (Barcelona). Author of **The Cabbie** (Catalan Communications: 1987) & other titles. "The Law" copyright © Marti, 1991. Reprinted by permission of the author.

FRANCIS MASSE (France). Author of the two-volume **Encyclopedia de Masse** (Les Humanoides Assoices: 1981) & other titles. "Public Utilities" copyright © Frances Masse, 1991. Reprinted by permission of the author.

JOE MATT (Toronto, Canada). Author of the forthcoming **AutoMatt** (Kitchen Sink: 1991). "My Parents" copyright © Joe Matt,1991. Reprinted by permission of the author.

LORENZO MATTOTTI (Milan, Italy). Author of **Fires** (Catalan Communications: 1989) & other titles. "Vanity Illustrations" copyright © Lorenzo Mattotti, 1991. Reprinted by permission of the author.

PAUL MAVRIDES (San Francisco). Co-author, with Gilbert Shelton, of recent issues of **The Fabulous Furry Freak Brothers** (Rip Off Press). "It Was Dino-Boy's Finest Hour" copyright © Paul Mavrides. Reprinted with permission of the author.

CAREL MOISEIWITSCH (Vancouver, B.C.). Author of **Flash Marks** (Fantagraphics). "Some Excerpts from The CIA Manual for Nicagagua" copyright © Carel Moiseiwitsch, 1991. Reprinted by permission of the author.

MOKEIT (Paris). Work has appeared in **LABO, Gin & Comics**, and numerous French underground comics magazines. "The Twiddlers" copyright © Mokeit, 1991. Reprinted by permission of the author.

JOSE MUNOZ (Milan). Co-author of **Joe's Bar** (Catalan Communications: 1989) & the ongoing comics magazine, **Sinner** (Fantagraphics Books). "34 Penn Station" copyright © Munoz & Sampayo, 1991. Reprinted by permission of the authors.

DIANE NOOMIN (San Francisco). Author of **True Glitz** (Rip Off Press: 1990). "What Big Girls Are Made Of" copyright © Diane Noomin, 1991. Reprinted with the permission of the author.

DAN O'NEILL (Nevada City, California). Author of **Farewell to the Gipper** (Eclipse Books: 1989) & other titles. "Belfast" copyright © Dan O'Neill, 1991. Reprinted by permission of the author's ancestors.

GARY PANTER (New York City). Author of **Jimbo: Adventures in Paradise** (Panthon: 1989). "The Roustabout" copyright © Gary Panter, 1991. Reprinted by permission of the author.

285

MARUO SUEHIRO (Tokyo, Japan). Author of the forthcoming graphic novel, **Mister Arashi's Amazing Freak Show** (Blast Books: 1992). "Bad" copyright © Maruo Suehiro, 1991. Reprinted by permission of the author.

JOOST SWARTE (Haarlem, Netherlands). Author of **Modern Art** (Real Free Press Foundation: 1984) & other titles. "The Adventures of Herge" copyright © Joost Swarte,1991. Reprinted by permission of the author.

JACQUES TARDI (France). Author of **Adele & The Beast** (NBM: NY, 1990) & other titles. "The Murderer of Hung" copyright © Jacques Tardi, 1991. Reprinted by permission of the author.

ROY TOMPKINS (Austin, Texas). Author of **Harvey The Hillbilly Bastard** (Fruit of the Tomb Publications: 1988). "Popeye Buddha" copyright © Roy Tompkins, 1991. Reprinted by permission of the author.

CAROL TYLER (Sacramento, California). Work has appeared in **Weirdo**, **Heck**, **Buzzard**, **Rip Off** and numberous other magazines. "Labor" copyright © Carol Tyler, 1991. Reprinted by permission of the author.

COLIN UPTON (Vancouver, British Colombia). Author of the ongoing comic book serial, **Big Thing** (Fantagraphic Books). "Stalingrad" copyright © Colin Upton, 1991. Reprinted by permission of the publisher.

CHRIS WARE (Austin, Texas). Author of **Floyd Farland, Citizen of the Future** (Eclipse Books: 1984). "Jimmy Corrigan" copyright © Chris Ware, 1991. Reprinted by permission of the author.

WILLEM, Bernard "Willem" Holstrop (France). Author of **Le Monde En Images** (Albin Michel: Paris, 1991). "Jerusalem" copyright © Willem, 1991. Reprinted by permission of the author.

MACK WHITE (Austin, Texas). Author of **Surreal Western Comics** (Metacomix: 1988). "Showdown at Rio Bobo" copyright © Mack White, 1991. Reprinted by permission of the author.

J.R. WILLIAMS (Portland, Oregon). Author of the ongoing comic book, **Bad Comics** (Cat-Head Comics). "The Quaalude Family" copyright © J.R. Williams, 1991. Reprinted by permission of the author.

ROBERT WILLIAMS (Los Angeles). Author of **Visual Addiction** (Last Gasp: 1989). "Hot Rod Tales" copyright © Robert Williams, 1991. Reprinted by permission of the author.

S. CLAY WILSON (San Francisco). Creator of **The Checkered Demon.** "The Bum & The Bird Spirit" copyright © S. Clay Wilson, 1991. Reprinted by permission of the author.

JIM WOODRING (Seattle). Author of the ongoing comic book magazine, **Jim** (Fantagraphics Books). "Frank and Manhog" copyright © Jim Woodring, 1991. Reprinted by permission of the author.

Y5P5 (Paris). Work has appeared in **Chemical Imbalance**, and numerous other international comic magazines. "The Job" copyright © Y5P5. Reprinted by permission of the author.

MARK ZINGARELLI (Seattle). Author of **Real Life** (Fantagraphics Books). "The Cockeyed Cook Story" copyright © Mark Zingarelli, 1991. Reprinted by permission of the author.

287